From Pen To Page

A biographical poetry collection

Blue Deco Publishing

www.bluedecopublishing.com

From Pen To Page

Cover by Colleen Nye
Editing by Alonzo Gomez, Colleen Nye & Wende Pepper
Layout & Formatting by Colleen Nye

Published by: Blue Deco Publishing
PO BOX 94 Potterville, MI 48876
BlueDecoPublishing@gmail.com

This work is a collection of biographical accounts and personal poetry. All names and situations mentioned are by the recounting of the poet and their perspective.

To my mother and step-father for teaching me that, in this world, you cannot simply exist – you must survive.

To my brothers for accepting me for the man that I have become.

To the women who tried to understand.

A note from Colleen Nye:

When Chacho, aka Alonzo Gomez, approached me about publishing his collection of poetry, I was surprised... and very intrigued. I love meeting people from various walks of life as well with various views of the world. And I believe talent can be found in some of the most unexpected places.

Through our chats, I became interested in knowing more about his colourful life and the intriguing man himself. It was an honour to be able to take his poetry and put it on the page, let alone having been able to take down his story as he tells it and shape it into the book you are about to read.

I hope you enjoy learning more about Chacho as much as I did.

And Wende... You are an invaluable part of this project. Thank you for all you have done to help bring it to life!

-Colleen Nye

Chapters:

1

Intro

When it comes to poetry, what do you picture? The 1970's coffee shop full of people snapping? A woman in colorful clothes and long hair anxious to tell you about her nature walk? The teenager full of angst, alone in their bedroom? How about the biker that's dressed in leather and covered in patches?

Allow me to introduce to you Alonzo Gomez, otherwise known as Chacho. He is that biker that you see in public and take a couple steps aside to let him walk by. He is that man that's done time. He is that poet you'd never expect. And I am that writer that's here to tell you his story as he tells it.

My name is Colleen Nye, and here is Alonzo's story...

Chapter One

The Youngster

Chacho was born February 9th, 1963 as Alonzo Gomez. He is the eldest of his brothers and one of many in their large, extended family. Born in Laredo, TX, his mother moved them to Olivet, Michigan, a small and quiet town, to keep the boys out of trouble and away from "bad crowds."

It wasn't long before they realized there were very few Mexican kids in the school. It wasn't rare to find that small of a percentage of minorities in towns like Olivet in the 1970's. Nor was it rare to find struggling families to be strong, stern and hard working.

That's how one could describe Alonzo's childhood... Stern and hard. The boys worked the farm when not at school. They helped the family earn what they got, but they didn't go without the basic necessities.

However, while Alonzo credits his mother for raising all four boys, his father was the main disciplinarian. He was tough on the boys. But when he was drinking, Alonzo's father became both physically and mentally abusive to the boys' mother. This abuse drove Alonzo's loyalties to side with his mother as well as become the self proclaimed protector of the family.

Eventually his parents' marriage would dissolve and end in divorce, but it was being brought up in a household with such disrespect and violence seeded a sense of confusion and anger in regards to love and relationships. It would prove to have a lasting effect on such a young man that would change the course of his life forever.

Before we delve into where his life went from here, let it be known that family is the element to life that Alonzo holds most dear to him. This shows in many facets including how he makes a brotherhood everywhere he's gone.

But it's his blood family – his mother and blood biological brothers – that are the closest to him. Despite stepping on cracks, stumbling on words and dropping the ball throughout his life, they are the largest root to his family tree... and the most important.

In poem, here's a glimpse of this aspect of his life...

DAY OF PAYMENT

Standing tall and head held high
I faced the judge
The jury returned its verdict
My hands formed fist

Sweat squeezed through my fingers
Life was rattled by a word
You have been found guilty!
Penalty begins with waiting

Emotional test are revived
What will be the sentence?
Currently not detained but deprived
Dreams become non-existent

Hearts left dangling
Courtroom strangled by silence
Tears could be heard hitting the floor
Friends and family went numb

Uncrossing fingers to wipe their eyes
I turned towards all of them with apologies
Pain and emptiness was revealed to all
Court then adjourned

I hugged and kissed loved ones
Walked out with pride
Defeated yet fought all the way

Though it hurts it's time to pay

Dedicated to: Mom, Tommy, Badger, Pooky, and Willie
12/13/87 - Sentencing day in Federal Court

MOMENT

To all who see me standing
My heart has fallen from within
Lying before me covered with sin
Who will help me at this moment?

Upon this picture focus your eyes
Remember it always, day and night
Turn back and follow a new path

I've just shown you true power
Hell and its torturing wrath
Who will help me at this moment?

Dedicated to: Tommy, Badger, Pooky
3/17/88

THE PAST

Taught God ruled and watched from above
Sharing with all his heavenly love
Listening to all by way of prayer
His power used to make life fair

He missed father busting walls
My prayers echoed through empty halls
Mother's tears unveiled her pain
Brothers asked for me to explain

Prayed when mother fell down the stairs
Waited for God to show he cares
Defended my brothers on drinking nights
Where the hell was God during those fights?

Most nights were filled with fear
Shouting and crying was all we could hear
After the echoes of shattering glass
Prayed for God to get off his ass

Father was big and very strong
Defense of mother never lasted long
Brother cried and didn't understand
When I'd hit the floor by father's hand

My courage was taught by mother
I refuse to give credit to that heavenly other
Father knew the past would not fade
He's tried to correct the mistakes he's made

My soul forever haunted by memories locked inside
Another victim of emotional genocide

Faith in God just drifted away
Forced to live life day to day

For me forgiveness may never come
Yes I've dealt pain to an innocent some
If I'd known the prices I would pay
In mother's womb I'd have chosen to stay

Forced to grow up so very fast
My future already infected by the past
Somehow, someway I've managed to survive
Five days out of seven I'm not even alive

If there is a God, lets' make a deal
Allow my family the love needed to heal
Then if you believe there's a price to be paid
Take my soul as the first payment made

Dedicated to my family
3/6/99

DEAR MOM, {A Mother's Day Letter}

It seems odd that I can express so many things through my poetry. Then it's almost impossible to express all the emotions and admiration I feel for you! As I write I picture myself as a person lost as sea. I can't remember how many times during my life you have thrown me a life preserver and keep me from drowning.

I do respect and appreciate the fact that once you had pulled me to safety you never stopped me from venturing again to the edge. I believe that's how I learned to survive and strengthen my confidence. I'm sure you thought that if you could stop me you could spare me tons of pain. Fact is those episodes helped create a man!

Never have I, nor will I, ever blame you for the cards life dealt me. I chose and created my own fate. My favorite quote says it best: "Ride in a carriage driven by Satan, only a fool asks the destination".

Thank you for teaching, by example, the strength to endure painful traps life laid before me.

Today we celebrate Mother's Day but every day of my life, in my soul, I celebrate this day out of love for you. You are my fountain of strength. When life becomes dry and I'm dying of thirst, I look to your fresh drink of hope.

The four letters that spell love could never express the thousands of different ways I love you!

If there is such a thing as reincarnation I would proudly return as your first born son again!

Your son,
Chacho

5/9/99

<u>BROTHERS</u>

Four brothers raised by one mother
All very different than one another
They all shared a mutual respect
For a loving mother they fiercely protect

Chacho, forty-two years of age
Filled his life with so much rage
Never turned his back on his brothers
Family always came before all others

Blaming no one for his path through life
Believed justice was found with a gun or knife
Feeling sometimes like he's not even alive
Thanks only his mother for teaching him to survive

Tommy is forty in age
Pursued a scripted life on stage
Allowing him to express emotions
In a language heard across the oceans

The first to move so far away
Gained strength with each character he played
Treated life as an audition
Yet never afraid to voice his position

Badger, third in line, age thirty-two
Would gladly give his last meal to you
With a heart bigger than all four
The kind of person God could adore

Always looking for a safe trail
For his family, any mountain, he would scale

Dear brother you fill us with so much pride
Never doubt, we're all at your side

Last but not least, at age thirty-one
State champion Pooky, Mama's spoiled son
He presented us with our first niece
As he learned about life piece by piece

Weathering a few storms of his own
Into a man he has grown
Still the closest to the nest
Draws from the examples set by the rest

Taught about life by one Mother
Learned to always care for one another
We should never stand alone
To face any stone thrown

Dedicated to Tommy, Badge, and "Pooky"
3/14/05

TO MOM

This apology is for you mother
I love and respect you like no other
Confused for words or where to begin
Impossible to count each and every sin

You tried to teach us that in God you believed
In my mind that idea was never conceived
You worked so very hard while raising four boys
Buying all of us new clothes and the latest toys

Every morning you sent us off to school
Wisdom told you, in life, education was a tool
I strayed beyond your protective reach
Then forced to learn lessons only streets can teach

Your bible says, for our sins, God's only Son had risen
Yet your oldest son followed a path to prison
Never blame yourself for my life that went wrong
Be proud that you taught us to always be strong

On occasion into the heavens I'll stare
Blaming God for burdens you've had to bare
You deserve the highest medal any angel can receive
For it is in you God should believe!

P.S. Thank you for being a friend and the greatest Mom.

11/18/06

FOR MY BROTHER

His tears fell like a silent rain
As bravery was swallowed up by pain
I held his hand and whispered we're all here
Mom said a prayer to help him with his fear

Her love surrounded him as he laid there
Two broken ankles, one beyond repair
I stood wish I could take his place
That those tears were running down my face

Thoughts of how he's always lived an honest life
Trying to build a home for his daughters and wife
It all just seems so unfair
My little brother, in so much pain, just lying there

God did you feel you owed my mother one
Wrapped your hands around her fallen son
You prevented a fatal wreck
By not allowing him to land on his back or neck

My recognition you do not need
Since my life the value of a weed
Thank you for not tearing mom's world apart
You've always had a spot in her heart

For her, please make everything okay
Sticking to our past agreement, I'll walk away
Never allow the skepticism we have for one another
Too ever cloud your reasons for protecting my mother and each
brother!

Dedicated to my Mom and Tommy
12/9/06

MOM MY SUNSHINE

In my cold and clouded world you're the sun
Teaching me that survival is more important than fun
Your rays of light and hope energize my soul
Giving me strength to pursue any goal

If the day starts slow and hazy
Your warmth keeps me from being sad and lazy
When everything is covered with ice and snow
With caution your light allows me to travel roads I know

Although we'd like to believe the sun will burn forever
Reality has allowed the moon to become very clever
With patience its dark cape shrouds the sun
A reminder life is not controlled by the force of one

If in my world the sun ever begins to fade
My path through life will be let by the prices she paid
With lessons I've learned, I'll sleep through the dark
To rise in the morning and create my own spark!

1/09

ANOTHER MOTHER'S DAY

To Mom,

I don't know how to begin the journey through my emotions that would express how deep my love for you is seeded.

I do know that when it rises to the surface, every empty space along the way is filled with the love and admiration you deserve. Not only as our mother but as a testament to all women who must ride the storm of single-motherhood.

As a teacher who thought by example that we should never quit or cower from a challenge.

As an advisor who believed there is always two sides to a story and any problem can be solved. To also stand behind the decisions you made.

As a disciplinarian, you believed some lessons required tough love, which must have been so painful at times but you knew (or at least hoped) it would allow passage to a new beginning.

As a friend who knew at times the best thing was just to listen. Then offering your opinion however soft or harsh.

As a coach who stood on the side lines of our individual games of life, not allowing us to dwell on defeat, but to learn from it.

As a nurse who put bandages and kisses on countless cuts and bruises. Yet, more importantly, you helped heal so many emotional wounds that all four of us experienced. Not one more important that the other.

Yet the greatest of all – as a mother. You took all those other examples and bound them together with an unconditional love. A security blanket for all four sons. For Pooky in his early father years and battle with alcohol, you helped develop a priority list. For Badge, when he was always so silent and never discussed his feelings, you taught him that emotions meant you were human and it was natural. For Tommy, who wandered so far away to pursue his career, you let him know that you were behind him 100% and that he could always come home. That helped him to build his confidence needed to succeed. For me my dear, you were the lion tamer. Knowing within stirred a beast, you had to try at the very least.

Mom, I love you.
Chacho

2012

Chapter Two

Finding Adulthood

Ok, so lets not get ahead of ourselves. Young Alonzo was just finding his way in the world. He was a child, already enduring quite a lot. But he was about to make choices that would shape his life forever.

In 9th grade, Alonzo joined the wrestling team at school. With a regular practice schedule as well as meets, wrestling became a good outlet for him to release his anger from his home life.

The young Alonzo excelled in the sport and quickly became captain of the varsity team. Not only did he take on wrestling, but he filled his days with other sports as well. Football and track filled in the weeks between seasons, keeping him busy and distracted. It helped that he was also considered one of the better linebackers his football team had.

His teammates treasured him since he was always there to stick up for the little guys. It seemed his protective instincts went past his home life. This was one of the assets that made him fairly popular with his class.

Alonzo's wrestling coach's guidance and training would have a lasting effect on the young man well into his adulthood. He learned lessons that would aide him in aspects he didn't even understand would come into play as a young man... and ones he never thought he'd have to face.

<u>COACH</u>

We stand here with respect and admiration
For a man that taught us the importance of preparation
That mind and body must operate as one
Then he'd ask, "Are you ready son?"

Never judging us by the loss or win
But were we as prepared as we could've been
In the coaches' chair his body sat
His heart, with each of us, in the center of the mat

I believe he's traveled with us beyond graduation
That little voice that reminds us about preparation
Work hard and give your all each day
Fearing no challenge that may stand in your way

Now we've gathered at the edge of your mat
What level of preparation are you at?
Looking back at all you've done
Well here it is, "Are you ready son?"

Dedicated to John Burton, wrestling coach 77 - 81
3/19/08

His grades were average, but he did the work and did his best. English and math were the topics he struggled with most, but his determination to make something of himself kept him pushing through it. However, sociology was not only his easiest class but his favorite. Learning the inner workings of the mind was fascinating and inspiring to him.

Alonzo graduated in 1981. After high school, Alonzo went to college for two years.

He attended Olivet College, having been recruited out of high school on a wrestling scholarship. And his major was in sociology and psychology, which would prove helpful throughout his life.

However, the partying and appealing aspects of having a social life and freedom being out on his own would prove to be too much temptation. He dropped out of college on the Spring Break of his sophomore year.

At first, he started working in construction. In and out of jobs in a traditionally seasonal work force, the down time allowed plenty opportunity for drinking. And drinking he continued to do.

But seeing what path it was taking him down and not feeling content in being stagnant in his life, he quit. It was a huge step and great insight for being only 23 at the time. And while those in his life saw it as a positive thing. It would prove to be the calm before the storm.

***

Once sober, a young and motivated Alonzo started working for his cousin as an enforcer in the drug business. He began to distance himself from his family to protect them from the dangers he was involved in on a daily basis.

Longing for something more, the lifestyle he was choosing was not only an adrenaline rush and a high he'd never experienced, it also allowed him to make a lot of money very quickly as well as make a name for himself. And for what he calls a short-cut in life, he figured this had to be his best chance. The best chance to rake in the dollars. The best chance to go places. And the best chance to be somebody.

He was taught to think and act like a soldier. His mentality was to get the job done as quickly and efficiently as possible, without regards to emotion. "It was a job."

However, those two years, ages twenty-three to twenty-five, proved to be two of the most difficult of his life. Thanks to the rise in turf wars, the job was not just dangerous, it was steady. And Alonzo was climbing the ranks quickly.

It was during this time that Alonzo found his voice in poetry, using it as a creative outlet in a world that was ruled by drugs and violence.

TEACHER

The darkness became my teacher
Enjoyed and used all I've won
Exploring the limits of darkness
Always avoiding the sun

Standing on the edge of day and night
Turn to my teacher with eyes full of fright
Only now can I add the cost
Of wounds that allowed emotions to be lost

I can see with the aid of light
The number of scars hidden from sight
No longer human but a nocturnal creature
I turn this time to question my teacher

Come as you will with physical threat
The damage is done, to my heart, my pet
Wounds that don't kill only make me stronger
The teacher, I need no longer

1984

<u>TEAR FROM HEAVEN</u>

High in our castle with permission to cry
Hands bleeding, they reach for the sky.
Dream clouds slowly go dark
Carrying the sound of a dogs bark.

It was not rain that just hit your hand
But tears from the one who created sky, water, and sand.
Clouds drift by with dreams we've lost.
Tears form as well as the cost.

Reach for illusions in a sorrow filled cell.
Not watching our step we tumble towards Hell.

1985

<u>RETURN</u>

Lay down your weapons
Come to me.
My chest will open for you to see
The scars defined upon my heart.
Suffered on the road to every new start.

I will never give in to physical pain,
In sight are objectives I will soon gain.
Down are my weapons
Entangled in an emotional war.

They physical armor has now become sore,
Must become stronger for this type of war.
The battles will never end,
I'll bare my chest when I return for more.

1985

<u>WAR</u>

With you challenges are great
Without you challenges are great
I am not an island
Battles I've won

The war rages on
Air begins to thicken
Enemies gather to unite
I stand to defend my ground

Reasons become blurry
In tears I face what comes
Drenched in sweat I hold them off
So they'll return

I radio for help
Can't anyone hear?
I have wounds to stitch
Blood runs nonstop

Will I last the next vicious charge?
I must wait and learn
At least know I tried
If I'm not here upon your return

1985

<u>GLORY</u>

Throughout my competitive years
I learned how to win
Played by the rules
Cheating was a sin

After each victory
Echoed the cheers of the crowd
Collecting my medals
I stood so proud

Life as a game has no rules
Referees are asses and fools
It hands us endless defeat
The arena silent without any sold seat

In this lifelong tournament
Don't be surprised if there are no winners
The finishers are survivors
Worlds greatest sinners

1985

WINDS

He sits and guards the others
They slowly move away
Frantic is the effort to keep them close
Not only to age is ability lost
There is the emotional cost

The time that should've been set aside
To check and strengthen knots.
His mind fills with wonder.
One by one strings slip from his hand.

Even with a grip that becomes tighter
Winds of change prevail.
Mind full of memories of anticipation
Filled each balloon.

Now taken by a force
From which there is no defense.
Winds, winds and winds.
Time, change, and knowledge.

1986

<u>Chapter Three</u>

A Loss of His Own

Alonzo found it difficult to maintain any sort of productive relationship as time went on. Love had become hollow and meaningless to him.

He had grown up without a positive role model to teach him how to treat a woman well. Coupling that with the betrayal he'd experienced, he found it impossible to trust anyone.

He found himself gruff and almost cold when it came to relationships. All the while, his feelings were raw when he did attempt to let someone in. This made him vulnerable to pain and disappointment from those he did.

In early 1987, Alonzo had found himself with a higher rank within his street gang and having to deal with what they had figured out was a leak. Someone was giving information of their activities to the authorities, and it was suspected that it was one of the officers' women.

Alonzo had been dating a young woman for about two years, and they'd gotten close with him keeping an apartment in California for when he was out there and in it full time. One afternoon, he'd had a heated discussion in the club house about the leak of information. He went to the apartment to discuss the matter with her.

Upon reaching the point in the conversation where he expressed his concern that one of the women was doing the talking, the young woman became agitated, accusing Alonzo of blaming her. And despite trying to stay calm and explain that wasn't what he was doing, her anger built.

Her final words to Alonzo were "This is why I will not raise our son in this."

When her last word was out, she launched herself over the sixth floor balcony. He ran after her, reaching out a moment too late. As his fingers grazed her hand, she fell to her death, killing not only herself but their unborn child.

Alonzo had not been aware that she was with child, nor would he father one at any other point in his life.

SON

Last night in a dream I finally met my son
He was trying to heal my pain from what his mother had done
Twenty-eight years I've kept his memory tucked away
My soul has been tortured ever since that fatal day

With his mother's smile there stood a young man
From my eyes then down my face, teardrops ran
Dad, I wanted to tell you that I know you tried
That when mom took me away part of your soul died

She shouted from the balcony "I'm carrying your son"
How can you be a father and someone's hired gun?
Dad I seen you running and calling her name
As mom stepped off the balcony leaving you the blame

You had her for a moment before she slipped from your hand
Angels gathered six floors below where we might land
I've never forgotten your face as farther away we fell
I'm speaking from heaven because unborn aren't allowed in hell

You walked past the gathering crowd without a sound
Dad the angels caught me, I never felt the ground
This true story must be so very hard for you to tell
As for mother, suicide is a sin. Penalty – eternal hell

Dedicated to my unborn son: Alonzo Alberto Gomez
9/25/15

Chapter Four

Prison

In 1987 many of those close to Alonzo, including his own cousin that had brought him into the life, turned on him. Competition and the hunger for power surpassed loyalty, and he became the target as they handed him over to the federal authorities.

Alonzo's case started within state, and he was looking at 1 – 3 years in prison with an option of parole. However, Luck was not on his side. The federal agents delayed his court dates long enough for new laws to take place that allowed them to view the case on a federal level. In that light, he was looking at a minimum f 4 years without an option of parole.

He was sentenced to five years in a federal prison.

The hardest thing for him was to see the look on his mother's face when the sentencing was handed down. The loss of freedom, the betrayal by so many he cared for, yes, that was all difficult enough. But it was the sorrow in her eyes that was almost too much to bear; that feeling that he had let her down. That was what hit the hardest on that day.

Loyalty had always been a word that meant a lot to him, but after a number of people he'd considered loyal had not only turned their backs on him but we're eager to hand him over, sending him to prison, his view on the concept of loyalty was challenged, and his trust was shaken.

While behind bars, he trusted no one. And writing poetry became something he used in place of friendships and therapists. His poetry served as both an escape from his surroundings as well as a way to work through the guilt he felt for the things he had done.

From sentencing, Alonzo was transported to a medium security federal prison in Milan, Michigan. The first stretch of time was served there and was less than eventful. But after a couple of months, he requested a transfer and was taken to the minimum security prison, Yankton.

In Yankton, located in South Dakota, he was able to be on work duty as well as serve in a location without fences. But after two years, he was ready to be closer to home again, and he was granted a transfer to Bradford in Pennsylvania.

Bradford was back to being in a medium security federal prison again, but it meant that he would be closer to his friends and family once he was released. The fact that it was in the middle of the Alleghany National Forest was a rather scenic bonus.

His time behind bars was not wasted. He started lifting weights while in Yankton and joined a power lifting team once he got to Bradford. And while he spent some of his time with other inmates, he kept an emotional distance from others, but he'd formed a group of friends that all had each other's backs when needed.

However, his closest friend while there was a man from the Hells Angels. And in that friendship, Alonzo learned more about the biker world and what it was all about...especially for a 1% club.

STRATEGY

The force gathers slowly behind me
One by one they fall into line
I shy away from this unsatisfied vine
Running blindly they fail to see
Blood runs rich with family loyalty
All others must move, he can just sit
Love can't be lost to a high priced bet
It is his mountain that has been created
Who gives the orders won't be debated
Mountains take shape with aid from all forces
Harnesses strapped only to strong horses
Those who can't pull the weight
Will never know what lies beyond the gate
Hearts calloused, scars we both bare
Reaching for dreams that aren't really there
Form lines and stand to fight
The guilt that hits you is not very light
Weight harnessed to me
With trust I wouldn't flee
Loyalty, love, and trust hold me together
To push for more space is not for the better
Be satisfied with the big three
You'll get your finest hour
You will stumble and fall
Pushing for money, lust, and power

1987

THE CLIMB

I sit on the side of a mountain
Resting my tired body and soul
Around me only clouds
As if to blanket me

Should I go back?
Stop this endless climb?
The path behind long yet conquered
Ahead a trail full of obstacles

Why think of turning back
To face hardships I've past?
I think only of the feeling
Reaching my goal at last

1987

MY RULES

Up or down
You must climb or fall
Day or night
Sleep through one, enjoy
Reverse or forward
Lose ground or leave it behind
Left or right
Take a turn, deal with it later
Good or bad
Choice is yours to live happy or sad
Black or white
Dark or concealed, on white all is revealed
LIFE or DEATH
Enjoy one the best you can, the other
Can't be stopped with any master plan.

1987

SEARCHING FOR LIGHT

I can see around me
Most have sight
What have I done blindly
With power and might

I've erased the days
Left only night
Lead me away
Take me to light

Hide from darkness and its fatal bite
Let me be lifted, like a wind driven kite
To shine in armor
With the praise of the knight

Before it is tarnished
With tears born to fright
For things only grow
Under sunshine and light

12/28/87

<u>CHILD OF THE DARK</u>

In darkness I was raised,
The chains still haunt my domain.
Power and money were all I praise,
Licking my wound and hit the pain.

Someone in a land far from here
Climbed on my shoulders and chased my fear.
Shadows were lifted, clouds moved away.
I couldn't believe the price I would pay.

To this day when I look at the sun
I think of my time out west.
Part of my heart stayed with one.
Who made the ultimate conquest?

12/28/87

<u>CHILDREN OF THE LESSOR</u>

Children of the lessor
This poem is for you
Through power and wealth
Was given only to few

Hang on to your love
You will gain riches they never knew
Only love bonds a person together
On our shoulder sits a dove

Judge people by their pages
Not by the cover
Hearts should not be in cages
Make life your most trusted lover

Through not forgiving but basic and true
Controlled by love not the powerful few
Hang onto love, it bonds us together
We have the dove, protect teach feather

12/30/87

EMPRESS

The empress smiles, thrown now hers
Her hands hold three keys
Card dealt her played with success
Not too proud to ask us for help

All here holding out hands
Don't drop the keys
They came only to take
Leave her something for God sake

The crown became tarnished and dirty
Waiting for a new son
Hold it just right the sparkles will return
Mind full of lessons
She was forced to learn

Gems in the crown cast beams of light
Images appear of three locks
Count the keys only she will use
Wet each key with a tear

We stand beside you, no need for fear
What's protected by each lock?
Sun will shine through our darkest hour
Three of the finest treasures
Love, Pride and Will Power

1/88

WHITE WAR

In the center of an eerie mist
A soldier leans on his weapon
As the natural blindness lifts
Bodies are revealed

Once soldiers
Once enemies
All started as friends
Casualties in a war that never ends

The frontline of this war
Is hidden within our souls
The screams of help
Are drowned out by laughter

There's no such thing as life after
Once drafted to this hidden war
There are no escapes
Through the ranks people move quickly
Directions given lead nowhere

There is no rank among the losses
Each body a victim to its own war
Decisions left to each soldier
There are no Sargents, Generals or Bosses

1/88

PEACEFUL CLOUD

In the distance a vision
Seen only by my eyes
The vision for which this lovely man cries
There is a shiny key

From my hands it's just out of reach
Will the chains of my past hold me back?
Can I build bridges over qualities I lack?

Give me a chance
I'll hold it proud
The key belongs to a heart
Peacefully resting on a cloud

1/6/88

CONQUEROR

Conqueror of life
Sitting upon a white horse of hope
Beware of sacrificing love for victories.
The support in your cause
May change to whispers of abandonment.
Your army will scatter.
Family, friends, and love will vanish into wilderness.
Surrounding your path.
Stay close in victory.
Join souls, hands, and mind.
Share all you learn and gain.
Alone you will parish!!!
The maggots of confusion will infest your mind.
Vultures then pick away your insides.
Finally with the scavenging finished,
The sun of loneliness dries skin and bleach bones.
Winds of change become stronger,
The sand of time cover our remains.
Another conqueror buried in a desert of lost souls!

1/27/88

LOOKING BACK

I add another year in age
Yet losing years of life
Life has changed me in so many ways
I'm not ready for a cage

Memories are spotted with happier days
Why did I choose such a life?
Answers accompanied by confusion
Once I dreamed of children and a wife

Must have been an illusion
Nobody can heal what makes me cry
Never pointing blame at others
I created my world with a lie

Forgive me please little brothers
Do not feel guilty anyone
With this confession and love,
I SAY GOODBYE

2/18/88

DECEPTION

In the distance looms a statue of gold
A landmark I followed through life
Hearing voices and sound I thought were cheers
Even in hazy days and foggy nights it stood bold

In one hand a heart and in the other a knife
Moving closer the sounds expressed fears
The statue symbolized lost love
Only fools' gold sparkled for years

In our race with life
Focus not on the sparkles of gold
Guard your heart from the hidden knife

3/17/88

CASTLE

A crystal castle I built
Reflecting all colors
It sparkled with life

Bumped from its pedestal
Shattered was life
Majestic powers scattered below

No powers or colors
What happened to life?
Gone the crystal castle I built

3/17/88

LOVE

I SAW
I WAS POSSESSED
I WANTED
IT BECAME MINE
I DEFENDED
IT BECAME SMOTHERED
I RELAXED
IT ESCAPED
I REACHED
IT DECEIVED ME
I LOVED
IT DEFEAT ME
3/18/88

SOLITARY MOMENT

Within four walls I sit and think
Surrounded by bodies left all alone
Inhaling air filled with criminal stink
Not very happy and I want to go home

Counting the wrongs I have done
Run out of finger, use also toes
Stopping to picture each one
Inside regret slowly grows

Time is now plenty
I grab another cigarette to bum
Friends are few
What a way to learn

Tell me I can't see
Is the sky blue
4/3/88

MOVING TOWARD THE LIGHT

For years I've hidden from the sun
In darkness I'd move as one
Thinking what next might go wrong
Sentenced to darkness for oh so long
I've lost love and friends
Hunted ideas that became dead ends
Moving aimlessly within my domain
Witnessed sorrow and pain
Reached the doors of freedom
An opportunity to emerge
Sunlight shines through the stairway door
No longer will I fear the light
Only my ghost will haunt the night
Mind, body, and soul will enjoy what's right

4/6/88

THE JOURNEY

Embarked on a journey
The course uncharted
No guarantee of a return
Filled with losses and lessons
I would be forced to learn

No more strength and lack of support
The journey has come to a sudden stop
I've run aground, sail torn and deflated
Never to see my original port

As I absorb the sudden stop
Will only my enemies remember me?
Friends forget my existence?
Mutiny by the crew

No longer am I the captain
Blame is passed quickly
Fingers point in all directions
The buck of blame is laid in my hand
It will travel no further
I guess this ship had only one man

4/10/88

FAMILY

Together we are a powerful family
We can shout our ideas and be heard
As individuals in this world
Advance kept distant, with speech whispered

In our blood Aztec pride
Rushing through a heart, soft yet protected
Motivated by conquistador courage
Look around brothers, we are nation wide

Armed with education, pride, and unity
Futures can only blossom identity
Together we are a powerful family

Aid your neighbor as you would a sister
Respect authority as you would a father
Love others as you would a mother
Defend them all like a Brother!

4/20/88

JUDGMENT DAY

Judgment day slowly approaches
I've become tense and bitter
Few loyalist remain close to me
Other hide like roaches

My words are harsh but not without reasons
They are leeches, beggars, and thieves
I'll gather the hunting party
Let loose the dogs of darkness

From them no one can hide
Thick is the armor across my back
From this direction the cowards attack
Gather the hunting party

I will not let them rest
Into their dreams I will ride
Greeting the heathens morning, noon, and night
The extermination of unwanted pests

I decide who is an enemy
Letting some believe they're friends
Making them such easy prey
I'll be judge, jury, and hangman
When it becomes their judgment day
I'LL SAY GUILTY!!!

4/27/88

ADMITTANCE WITH A LIE

The question is asked
With a show of hands
Who's the man?
Voices from all directions shout
I am. No I am.

A display of scars
War stories stretched
Laughter fills the room

Admitting who we've done
Pretending it's all in fun
Rulers of the darkness
Are we tough without the gun?

So many confessions
Count the lies
Alliances discussed
Loyalty a must

Some boasts "he's like a brother"
Remember Cain and Abel?
They hated one another

5/6/88

FRIENDLY SILENCE

Sitting with my newest friend
Remembering loving moments
Shadowed by tarnished memories
My chin begins to drop

From smile to frown
Hands keep my chin from reaching the ground
Asking my friend "what is the answer?"
Wishing to forget the past

Awaiting a reply
My friend doesn't answer fast
I've tried to solve the problem
Not without help

Again asking, still no answer
Asking for guidance
Briefly the conversation lasts
The reason I get no answer
My friend is silence!

5/7/88

TOMORROW

Lost track of tomorrow
Was it ever there?
Dreams are made for tomorrow
Is it still out there somewhere?

Standing waiting for a sign
Tell me it soon will return
I've looked everywhere
Should I form a new dream?

Base it on yesterday?
Should I forget dreaming? Live only for today?
For without tomorrow
I can dream only of a cure

To heal my pain created by sorrow
Lost track of tomorrow!

5/15/88

<u>BOOKS</u>

I sit in the library of life
Searching for a book
One which would ease my mind
Like most I was drawn to the cover

Full of color and glamour
I took it into my hands
Slowly I looked it over
I began to read

I realized the story didn't match the cover
Slammed it closed
Found the cover had been switched
Help to draw attention

The book was like all others
Introduction, plot, and ending
I returned it to the shelf
Someone else might enjoy it!

5/15/88

LISTEN FRIENDS

To those people who say they care
The weight of this wish is not easy to bare
I ask that pity not be poured out for me
That tears be hidden from my sight

I understand the rules of this arena
Yet, I do not run, here I stand
If you truly feel for me
Lend me your hand

Check my leather and shine my armor
Buckle every belt
Tighten each strap
Lay a heavy sharpened sword upon my lap

Cheer for me and drain each lung
Build my courage like never before
Pride will flourish when my blade is swung
Continue cheering and clapping

These sounds form the exit door
Dreams of the future place into my dish
Only true friends can grant this wish

6/19/88

<u>HONEST OFFERING</u>

To my friends who remain on the streets
Not much do I have now to offer
Advice is now plentiful and free to give
I only wish to make life, for you, easier to live

I know all too well it's hard to accept
Slowing down takes great effort
To reach the clouds, you must climb existing hills
Beyond them the majestic mountains

Do not waste time trying to stand alone
Prepare yourself for torturing consequences
Tears will form fountains
Scars will reach down to the bone

Relationships divided by barbwire fences
On your own ego do not feed
Listen and learn, wisdom you'll earn
Of course if you know it all there's no need

6/26/88

KINGDOM

The kingdom has finally vanished
Protective walls have crumbled back to Earth
Rulers gone and defeated
Guards forever banished

Destruction started inside the walls
Threats led to a lack of trust
Plans of betrayal to further wealth
The shiny kingdom is now covered by dust

The importance of secret meetings
Fed doubt to the minds that attended
Who could be trusted?
Alliance and loyalty are extended

Rulers and soldiers have no armor that shines
Memories flicker with what could've been
History repeats itself
Another kingdom is covered with vines

8/10/88

<u>A FORM OF CONFESSION</u>

Eyes RED and full of tears
Defeated by the world I built
Her crying sparked by fear
I sit alone confused by guilt

She said "I'm Sorry! You'll survive."
Emotional wounds ripped through my heart
I only looked alive
Inside I slowly fell apart

Wounds became infected with loneliness
The stench of my past filled the air
I watched her inhale a breath
She began choking and I just stood there

My veins began to dry
Blood replaced by pain
Offering no help, she had learned my art
To be bold and callus, to show no heart

11/16/88

SCAVENGERS

The sun begins receding from the sky
Darkness blankets souls I once controlled
Eyes of jackals glow like lasers
Wanting to enjoy the spoils of my victories
Laughter from hyenas shatters the silence
Being so lazy, when feeding themselves
They enjoy feeding on the weak
Those confused about whose protection to seek
Enjoy while you can scavengers
Take notice, I have no boundaries
Fearing no challenge I come and go at will
Moving through day and night
Keep the leftovers
I've had my delight
Vultures will form a circle of despair
An invitation for all to come a little closer
So you too can feel my fatal bite

12/16/88

CRY

Cry, cry, cry.
If I only could.
Tears just won't fall
As I know they should.

Run my hand across my face
I feel leather not satin or lace.
Skin that has become tough,
Thanks to a life that only played rough.

Someone believe me, inside there is a charm
I was not born for vengeance and harm
Disregard each ugly scar
I too wish upon a shiny star;

1989

WHERE ARE YOU NOW?

Where are you now?
I can't seem to find you
Don't look so surprised my dear
This poem is just for you

Masks you've worn have served their purpose
I was blinded and totally fooled
My heart fell victim to your hollow words
"I love you" and "I'll always be there"
Never and always come as a pair

Those words allowed passage to my soul
Now forced to cling to tender moments
Questioning their true value
Who is at fault? Me or you?

A mask to say goodbye
Why avoid me?
With all your masks
Don't you have one that answers why?

Teach me the secret you display so well
Pretending to be in heaven
While putting someone through hell

Enjoy the bar and your real friends
When I reach my bars
For your enjoyment my life ends

PS. Thanks for being there. I Love You. Oh ya, Happy New
Year!

Dedicated to Cyndi
1/2/89

<u>OFFERINGS</u>

I offered my hand,
You avoided my touch.
I offered roses,
You wouldn't smell them.
I offered secret fruit,
Closed your mouth without a taste.
I offered words of love,
You covered your ears.
I offered my heart,
Calloused hands held it for you to see
You closed your eyes and refused to believe.
I then fell to my knees
Tears ran down my face
I had finally fallen from your grace!

Dedicated to Cyndi
1/7/89

DECISIONS

Justified for wanting a better life
Invading any battle ground
Giants fell in defeat
Outnumbered, still gained victory
Charging upon a stallion of deceit
In constant pursuit of power
Search for a finest hour
Castle vulnerable by distance
Blackbirds entering, offered lies
Deceiving the queen with jealous words
Not listening to truthful heartbeats
Mounting her white mare of guidance
Vowing never to return, she vanished into winter
On my knees before an empty castle
Holding the stallion of deception
Staring into his fiery red eyes
Slowly taking aim, raising my sword
Strength of ten men filled my arms
Down the sword
Off with his head
Steam surrounded our bodies
Armor lay in snow now colored red
On foot with tears frozen, following her trail
Lost my last battle, couldn't prevail
I command no army
Searching for a safe region
Her Arms

1/7/89

KEEPERS OF THE ZOO

Come look and see the animals
That live and sleep and do
Everyone has a constant fear
Of the keeper of the zoo

Each of us knows what we are
Do we truly belong here in this zoo?
They're always keeping watch it seems
For the keepers of the zoo

Just as keepers always will
They attempt to break us, it's true
The will of most seems so very weak
To the keepers of the zoo

Late at night still flow the tears
Deep pain for all is so very true
Human feelings matter not
To the keepers of the zoo

One can't help but wonder
If all we're told is true
Is this life simply an illusion?
With the animals watching you

One day will ring our freedom bell
The caged up time is through
Then we'll wave and say farewell
To the keepers of the zoo

Off to find the place called home
To laugh and live and do

The only ones to stay behind
Are the keepers of the zoo!

3/91- About Prison

Chapter Five

From One Darkness To Another

On June 17, 1992, Alonzo was released from prison. But his time hadn't taught him what the court had intended. It had not instilled in him a sense of remorse or the knowledge that his choices had been wrong. Instead, what he learned from his time there was the ability to carry a no-nonsense view towards people in general.

However, one good lesson Alonzo had re-instilled in him was the value of someone's word. It was a virtue that he's prized when he was younger that had been reinforced in his mindset while looking at the world from behind a set of bars.

Through reflecting upon his own actions as well a listening to other inmates recount their own experiences and the issues so many others had before going behind bars; life lessons had engrained a sense of honor in Alonzo that would stick with him the rest of his life. Loyalty and keeping one's word became so important to him, and through the years that followed, he would uphold that value with an iron fist.

However, no matter of reforming that prison was supposed to provide, it wasn't long before he found himself in deep within the drug business again. He also started riding motorcycles as well, finding more and more avenues to get himself entangled with dark and dangerous avenues of life.

Door after door opened up to him as he maintained his cold, all-business type of demeanor. It wasn't hard for him to gain respect from those that saw he wasn't out to gain anything he wasn't able to earn for himself.

Quickly, he found himself directly in the mix where the drug world meets motorcycle clubs ... The part of the world most people only see on television. And it was a place where Alonzo saw an opportunity to not only finally make a name for himself but also attain the power he'd been looking for.

No matter how much power or how many people knew his name (which, incidentally had changed to "Chacho" as those in the MC's do not go by their real names) he never gave up his poetry, finding that it not only helped him with his past, but it also was a key element to making it through his present.

And the next several years would serve to be a time that he would need to do a lot of reflecting.

67

TO A FRIEND

Don't say a word, just hold me
Let your hands ask the questions
Kiss me to find your answers
With your eyes untangle my emotions

Don't say a word, just hold me
Never wake me from this dream
Lie next to me and make it last
Feed me your innermost secrets
Tasting what gives your energy

Don't say a word, just hold me
Never stop me from living on the edge
If I fall from your hands, kiss, and eyes
Keep whatever is felt, tasted, and seen

Don't say a word, just hold me
Taking with me the softness of your kiss
The warmth of your touch
The power in your eyes
The taste of your secret
Don't say a word, just hold me

Dedicated to Alyse
1993

ADDICTION

Looking in the diary of my mind
Flowing through the cracks of my memories
At night I pick you from my brain
Hands covered with blood
They chase you in and out of my heart

Filling me like an addiction
Fire and ice both flow through my veins
Tearing away my flesh
Allowing you access to my soul
Making overdose and art

Searching for that rare fix
Beyond anyone's idea of control
I have tasted the pleasure
Experienced the beautiful high

I'll lay me down to sleep
Waiting on that ghost
To inject my mind with your nakedness
Addicted until the day I die!

Dedicated to Alyse
11/6/93

<u>WHIPPING POST</u>

What did I do so wrong?
Tied me to the whipping post
Torture lasted so long
No escape for even my ghost

Picked my skin from under your nails
Dried my blood from your whip
Your witches enjoyed my wails
Destroyed my heart strip by strip

You laughed when I finally cried
Never thought I'd die so hated
Said you loved me but you lied
Hanging from the whipping post is what you CREATED!

4/20/94

ON THE ROAD

The flame danced into my eyes
Teasing my soul from all directions
Ran the red light of realistic dreams
Slid right through the emotional intersection

Nonstop down Alyse Avenue
Made the turn without looking
Never seen the warnings
Speeding all night, slowing down for day

It's a one way street
I'll never know where it ends
Traveling so blind
Couldn't bring my friends

No exit from the one way trip
Racing into the future, mind off track
Slamming into a wall, lost my grip
My heat was the price
Tortured soul thrown back

The wolf represents lonely life
Chained near the scene of my death
Howling in pain caused by my fatal mistakes
Only wanted to love you for God sakes

Dedicated to Alyse
5/9/94

CLOSED MIND

In her anger
Vengeance dances in her eyes
Needing only herself
Her words will never lie
Circled by walls of protection
No one is allowed inside
No one leaves alive
Believing not a single man
She has faith only in her pride
Save your words
You've been found guilty
In her mysteriously closed mind
She'll just turn her back
Leaving you far behind!

9/94

D.O.A.

SEE YOU IN HELL
THE PRICE OF LOVE
LOVE IS A LIE
ARE YOU FINISHED
LIVE, LOVE AND DIE
IN THE NAME OF LOVE
THE END
HAPPILY EVER AFTER
TOY OF LIFE
D.O.A.

9/9/94

A VICTIMS MEMORY

Alone in the dark
Mind and emotions decay
Her poison entered my heart
All used up, throw me away

Vengeance dances in thought
It would only be fair
Lying words of love
How could you ever care?

Defend God, love and faith
Is this what you learned?
Opened like sacrifice
Insides then burned

Raped my soul
That made you smile
Lied about love
Believed you for awhile

Truth has arrived
Needed your space
For beer, friends, and party
Back to leather and lace

Awake night after night
Thought travel far
Turning your back
To spend life in a bar

Thought you needed me
Just another lie
I'm sure you're laughing
Wishing I would cry

I hope your tears
Carve rivers in your face

You sent me to hell
I'll wait for my ace

Darkness is talking
Return to me my son
She believes in God
He gave her the gun

Your words have no value
Lies from within
Awaiting you in hell
A dead man with a grin

My whispers will slice your silence
Ghosts will haunt your mind
Scrub away my torch
My demon stays behind

Love is only venom
Burning through every vein
There is no cure
It drive all men insane

I'll wait down in hell
For the end of the game
Planning your reception
Only yourself to blame

Walking on victims
Your acting so high
My arms reach for you
Can't wait for you to die

I'm sorry my dear
These words come from hate
Fools who believe in love
Death is their fate.

1995

THE HUNTED

Once the hunter, I became the hunted
Lying in retreat licking my wounds
Leather skin stood no chance
Sliced by the serpent's razor tongue
Paralyzed by her beauty
Venom entered silently behind her kiss
Spitting blood, I could not cry for mercy
Emotions began to rot away from my soul
The serpent had found me guilty
Violations of trust and lack of attention
God and his angels turned backs to my prayers
Satan's eyes burned with evil as he laughed
Demons decorated my cell with loneliness
A smile and deception sliced away my heart
Feasting on the spoils of her recent victory
Spitting away pieces of memories
Savoring the warm life blood
Convicted of violating her rules
My soul imprisoned by demons
The heart offered affection but was devoured
Veins were drained to moisten her lips
Sealing my mouth, eyes, and ears
I became an emotional zombie
Alone in a false resurrection
Thought of the burning lessons
Principles I failed to learn
Yes Queen Serpent, you reign supreme
The outcome will be different upon my RETURN!

1/17/99

A FOOLS DREAM

Vultures gather watching love die
Tears fall slowly only to dry
Soaring high waiting to descend
Silently enjoying another fools end

Another victory for wrong over right
Dreams of love are way out of sight
All eyes focus on the broken heart
Taking pleasure in tearing it apart

Ripping out eyes that once cried
Dancing in blood that skin use to hide
Each piece of flesh is a memory gone bad
Ending all dreams the fool might have had

Desperately picking the bones clean
Soon arrives darkness, world of the mean
Gather the demons sharing one goal
Arriving with smiles to torture the fool's soul

Forced to return to the world below
The fire in hell has a familiar glow
Blinded by love placed my neck in a noose
Once again it was Satan who cut me loose

Standing empty with demons at my side
I have no fear, been on this ride
Ideas of vengeance dance in my head
Cursing the world awaiting it's dead

Fools believe love is fed by hope
Only to be found kicking at the end of a rope
Vultures then return to the smell of death
Demons await the fools' last breath

Satan uses Love as a fools bait
Luring them in before they realize it's too late
It's too bad, In dreams of Love, fools believe
Only to find it's where hate is conceived

2/20/99

A SECRET

Late at night they come alive
Through my dreams they arrive
Escapees from a shadowy past
Lives disrupted by a shotgun blast

Never asking the reasons why
No one to hear their final cry
Secrets that will never be revealed
Their lips now forever sealed

Memories that were locked away
Have escaped to make me pay
Lives that were ended with an envelope
One by gun and one by rope

Three can keep a secret if two are dead
They remain buried in my head
Reminders that secrets are never over
Until all three are covered with clover

2/9/02

ONE LAST PROMISE

Here's a little promise brought on by hate
Step aside demons I'm running late
I've had enough of this life it bores me
It's the other side I want to see

At a hundred miles an hour I want to go
To the center of HELL where fires glow
My number has been called and it's about time
I've been haunted by each foolish crime

Fell victim to love, It's only a lie
It can cause the strongest man to die
I can't wait until it's your turn
I'll be laughing as your soul begins to burn

If my demons catch you alone
No holy water will be thrown
Not even gonna waste my spit
One last promise: I'll keep the fire in Hell lit

3/2/03

LOOSING TEN YEARS

Alone while darkness arrives
Wishing I had a cat's nine lives
Tortured the life I was given
For that I'll never be forgiven

Emotion and guilt lost along the way
Victim of loneliness day after day
Drug no longer heal the pain
Pretending to laugh while going insane

Allowing no one to hear me cry aloud
Always alone even in a crowd
Ten years of life just walked away
Loneliness seems so willing to stay

Look deep into my eyes
My soul wants you to see its goodbyes
Now my heart sits empty and cold
Its blanket of dreams has been sold

7/28/03

TO ALYSE

To my Alyse, I wrote this poem
In your hand my hearts at home
Every minute that fills a day I miss you
Making each day almost impossible to live through

I have no clue how it came apart
Even my worlds don't know where to start
Wish I could turn back the clock
To soften this heart made of rock

Emotions eroded from my soul
Makes finding love a distant goal
Grasping for memories with my force
Without you I've gone off course

It's so hard to swallow blame
In your eyes my external flame
Please stop pushing me away
I want to love you till my dying day

12/03

THE ILLUSION

Now reaching my later years
Dreams give way to silent fears
That all the memories of my past
May be shattered by love that never lasts

Cheated out of emotions at a young age
Only to spend years locked in a cage
Tried to find my one and only true love
In this crazy world of push and shove

At times believing I'd found the one
Before they started, they were done
The times that joy would fill my heart
Made it vulnerable to be torn apart

I have only myself to blame
Thinking that life was just a game
Over the years I've become set in my ways
Thoughts of love lost in a haze

Do not let it become a surprise
That the heart will also tell you lies
Just when you think love is going to stay
With your soul and emotions, you will pay

2/18/05

TO MY FRIEND OF OVER 20 YEARS

Not just a friend but a brother
Trust my life with no other
Twenty-four years have passed us bye
You told me the truth when others would lie

Spent most of your life giving
All the while trying to stay living
Your children are always first
Protecting them from hunger and thirst

We've both traveled the lost highway
As we took life day to day
Looking for shelter of any kind
While searching for our own peace of mind

When I was drinking everyday
You told me I was letting life slip away
Now eighteen years without a drop
Thank you for the incentive to stop

Then sent to prison full of fears
You encouraged me throughout those years
Helping me upon my return
Didn't let me crash and burn

My loyalty is never at stake
No matter what risks we must take
I'd stand back to the wall for no other
I feel proud when you call me brother

The future hold secrets we don't know
Say the word and I'm ready to go!!!

Dedicated to the original 88 - my friend Gary
2/20/05

I HAVE A HELLBOUND HEART

I have a hell bound heart
World has been blown apart
Missing my only friend
Now at wits end

I have a hell bound heart
Wishing for a new start
Veins fill with sorrow
Not looking forward to tomorrow

I have a hell bound heart
Made loneliness an art
Happiness I have not found
Destination hell bound

3/5/05

SPEAKING TO ALYSE

What day is it today?
One too many that I've been away
Knowing damn well at day's end
I'll be missing my only friend

Thoughts wrapped so very tight
As Clapton sings "You look wonderful tonight"
Thinking of all the things I've done
Forced to face the world as one

Gone are emotions once kept inside
At days end so is my pride
Only your touch helped heal the void
Where once was a heart that life and prison destroyed

Overlooked the hidden costs
Of allowing my soul to wander lost
I hope someday I'll find my way back
To putting my life back on the right track

Allow me to follow the fire in your eyes
I'm asking you before my soul dies
You must believe what I say
I'm dying inside, soul bleeding each day

I don't know what you want to hear
That I can't stand to look in a mirror
Once I was full of pride
Lost it all when love died

Sorry that tears just won't fall
Can't seem to cry at all
Pain wishes but can't escape
Heart feels like a victim of rape

Please allow me to apologize
For all the tears I left in your eyes
Wishing I could wipe them dry
To once again see the sparkle in each EYE!

Dedicated to Alyse
3/14/05

THE GLANCE

With only a momentary glance
Defense stood absolutely no chance
Walls that had stood solid for ages
Opened, like a book, revealing hidden pages

She stepped softly between the lines
Never missing any warning signs
I couldn't even sound the alarm
Ambushed by stealthy charm

Tools that consisted of eyes and smile
Left my four walls in a crumpled pile
Then secretly settling my fears
Made me feel like a friend of many years

Our discussion had a peaceful flow
As a rare friendship began to grow
To avoid telling a malicious lie
Must admit, I didn't want to say goodbye

Words spoken are locked safely inside
A rule by which I firmly abide
Each day that follows, allows at least one thought
Of a special moment that could never be bought

Dedicated to a special woman
3/21/05

<u>REGRET</u>

Sitting alone at eleven o'clock
Thoughts of you accompanied by tick-tock
Tried to reach you by phone
Here comes another night alone

Too many nights to even count
Feelings of madness continue to mount
In your arms it was kept at bay
Their protection now so far away

Whispering the words "It will be alright"
I kiss your picture every night
Wishing I had never made you cry
You file my apologies under the word lie

Now I lay me down to sleep
No one in the world must hear me weep
Polished the mask I'll wear tomorrow
Yes, the one that covers all my sorrow

Once again I'll survive the day
With my pain hidden far away
Confused by thoughts of what to do
My words "I LOVE YOU" are so very true

Dedicated to Alyse
4/7/05

<u>AWAKENED ALONE</u>

Once again I'm alive, disappointed by a breath just taken
Face another day in this life so forsaken
Hate to open my eyes because no one is there
An emptiness so far beyond repair

I would kneel and beg on shattered glass
If my life would be allowed to pass
Silently and forgotten, to the other side
Since life is now void of my only friend and pride

To create tears was never my intention
Burn in hell, you outsiders, creating all the dissension
Hope your loved ones rot and die
Feel my pain when she said goodbye

Think I loved you before I was born
I'll love you even when from life I'm torn
Never allowing one memory to burn
For when I'm scared and lonely that's where I return!

8/4/05

LAST GOODBYE

People file by looking down at me
Wish their face I could see
Eyes begin to overflow with tears
Finally freedom after all these years

Each person reaches out to me
Only to find I'm as cold as can be
The Tinman never found a heart
Now it's too late and time to depart

Let her who may have loved me last
Join the pretenders of my past
Feeling no love at the very end
I became my only friend

Wondering why I must go
My mother crying out "no, no, no"
The little boy she tried to teach
Would now be placed beyond her reach

Allow only my brothers to carry me home
Polish my headstone made of chrome
Please wipe away my painted smile
Life for me has been painful for a while

To those who have ever wished me dead
I'll be waiting and making your bed
Remember, no matter how long it may take
You, in life, will also make a fatal mistake

12/1/05

89

DREAMS

Thinking about some dreams I've had
Most of which turned out bad
In their background wasted time
Vacant of love but filled with crime

So many years have passed me by
All alone, my own fault, living this lie
Vivid in color but lacking sound
Standing alone on blood soaked ground

Life now blurry as it passes by
Yet clear are visions where two bodies lie
Some show friends dead or locked away
Always showing me alone then and today

Physical strength replaced with pride
Can't keep grip of this emotional ride
I fear the dream with a distant hell
Belonging not to a church but the elevator of Hell!

3/11/06

MENTAL FOG

Welcome to another night alone
Emptiness has turn another heart to stone
Dreams fog my mind, awaiting their turn
To display memories of my last crash and burn

In a state of confusion, what should I do?
Can't remember the sound of I love you!
Reached this point I don't know how?
The whole damn world looks distant now!

Desperately wishing you'd take me back
But the crazy train won't stay on track
Just when I feel that I'm well on my way
I'm once again lonely at the end of the day

I believe this is what you consider fun
Breaking the heart of another mother's son
Mind and heart are of no use to you
Scraps left floating in your witches brew!

Dedicated to Alyse
5/5/06

GOD'S CHEATING

Slammed into the weeping wall
God's trying to take them all
Should've know he'd cheat at the end
Doesn't matter what rule he has to bend

First he created a canyon between love and I
Erasing the sparkle she had in each eye
She now turns her head with shame and discuss
Love has vanished or died like trust

Second, mother's being forced to age too fast
Holding her prayers hostage because of my past
She's always believed in God to heal emotional thirst
Yet it seems, that he has often punished her first

Third, pulled my best friend into their sight
Another victim of the war between wrong and right
Only a man out there trying to survive
Whey send his world into a vertical dive

Here's a message I'd like to send
Who's God? Satan's been more of a friend
Why pick on people so close to me?
Oh, can't come off the porch and still squatting to pee!

6/10/06

<u>SURVIVAL</u>

The lonely search for love is not a living
People will always take and take, till you stop giving
Each hug becomes tighter than the last
Here come the memories of a dominated past

Heart divided into four equal parts
Clothing fills every laundry cart
Three daughters and a son
Trying to make life for them fun

Freedom can feel like a ball and chain
When it is inhaled without restrain
You survive the years of transition
To place your children in a starting position

Blindsided by the direction marriage would take
Fooled by true love that was actually fake
Eight plus years of feeling less than zero
Rewarded by four success stories that will call mom the Hero!

Dedicated to Jessica
6/11/06

ABYSS

Alone staring into an Abyss
Thinking of the precious people I miss
Few moments have ever warmed my soul
Life has taken a terrible toll

Guilty of creating victims, enemies, and no friends
With wishes, regrets, and revenge and the day ends
My true love went off and married
Snitches still walking and should be buried

The only friend I could trust is still there
Just don't remember all the grey hair
Thankful for the times he stood at my side
Otherwise I may not have survived the ride

I've been told my eyes look empty and cold
That's because everything inside has been sold
It's true wisdom we must earn
First my friends you must survive the crash and burn

9/14/06

<u>FACES</u>

Once upon a time we could smile
Laughing our way through every last mile
Time has painted over faces with sin
Smiles have changed into a devilish grin

Said to have faces cut out of stone
With eyes that are dark, empty and alone
Suspicious minds that allow no trust
Protecting hearts now covered with dust

Eighty miles an hour and still side by side
Cleansing our souls with the wind as we ride
No destination ever really in sight
Sometimes just riding until it was light

In the darkness our reputations were made
Unable to add the prices we've paid
Wishing only to be left alone
Let he who is perfect cast the first stone

11/18/06

OUTSIDE MY DOOR

Once again without you near
Loneliness will soon appear
My soul prepares for what's in store
The gathering of demons at my door

Never knowing how long they'll stay
It's so very hard to keep them away
Arriving with memories from the past
They'll shred my soul like a shotgun blast

Dancing with joy because I've been caught alone
They begin cutting my soul from bone
Feeding on my emotions with an evil smile
Hoping loneliness decides to stay awhile

Inside this war will rage but won't be seen
One I may lose if my soul is picked clean
When the smoke clears from the battleground
The echoes of your name will be the only sound

11/23/06

Chapter Six

What Goes Up Must Come Down

At the age of 44 (2007) Alonzo joined a 1% motorcycle club. Their reputation regarding how they ran their members matched his own style of iron fist ruling. There was no question that he would not only fit in but excel within the environment.

Over the next several years, he worked his way through the ranks. Sergeant of Arms, Master Sergeant, Vice President and President were some of the positions he held in one of the most powerful chapters of one of the more influencing 1% clubs in the U.S.

However, approaching time for his second term as president for his chapter, Alonzo would feel the sting of betrayal once again. After eight years of dedication to the club and his brothers, another member had been working towards setting themselves up with a situation that allowed not only themselves to take Alonzo's place but also push him completely out of the club... costing him not only his station but also his "man-made family".

Alonzo had been completely blind-sided by the decision. He had not had any indication that his loyalty was being questioned by his brothers, nor had he known that his heavy-handed approach to handling situations was causing any unrest. But he soon found out that there had been on-going talks behind closed doors.

What he learned was that one man made severe accusations and convinced others of situations that were not entirely true. And when Alonzo tried to step forward to shine the truth on the situation, including to offer to pay for lie detector testing for his accusers, he was met with a stone wall of unforgiving club members.

In the end, three other men were relieved of their stations and stripped of the badges. And Alonzo walked away knowing that he did what he could, but in the end, he knew he still had his dignity and respect in tact. He didn't stoop to anyone's levels in trying to force people to see the truth in the situations. And he could walk away, proudly, from the situation knowing he had the truth on his side.

After his uneasy split from the club, he stayed in touch with old club brothers as well as having been in touch with a number of other clubs. He's not made any steps towards joining any in particular, befriending bikers from various clubs and even independent. But what he knows is that he's not going to be sidelined and gun shy. He's going to stay true to himself.

BIRTHDAY

The clock finally struck midnight, turned forty-four
My best friend stretched out on the floor
Looking up at me wanting to play
Hell, for him, this was just another day

No cards, presents or even a dinner
Another birthday in the life of a sinner
One by one family members call
Shattering the silence of each surrounding wall

Sending their love and wishing me the best
Sorry no party, not even one guest
Never thought I'd live this long
My best days, I believe, have come and gone

Yet with a smile, I just went to bed
Their word of "I Love You" still echoing in my head
Off to dreamland I begin to drift
Having my family will always be the greatest gift

2/9/07

THE FIRE

In an instant all was gone
Watched it burn from the neighbor's lawn
Everything I owned went up in flames
Harley Davidson to some old word games

Inspecting a sound that seems out of place
Suddenly flames flashed toward my face
Shirt began to burn, felt the heat
Thinking my maker I would soon meet

Turned to face the fiery beast
Save the Harley, try the least
The fire forced me to retreat
My treasure burning and I regretting defeat

My poor dog didn't understand
Dragging him violently by the collar in hand
Desperately searching for fresh air
Surround by the smell of burnt hair

Once again slammed to the ground
Looks like God won another round
Revenge for something I've done
Or do you still consider me Satan's son!

2/25/07

NO GOOD NEWS

In a small room across town
Flooded by sorrow and about to drown
I write the words that are haunting my head
As my dog rest peacefully on my bed

Once again forced to rebuild my life
Sorrow cuts with loneliness as its knife
I can only pretend to be so strong
At war with a life that's gone so wrong

I hear laughter from the pretenders
I've heard encouragement from my defenders
It's been said "What goes around, comes around"
Allow only me to put their laughter in the ground

I want the chance to turn my back
To forget a call or even help them pack
To walk away from the fake friends
To enjoy the moment their world ends

Yes, it is all about me
I'll step up, I don't squat to pee
Cutting them all out of my life
Demons have sharpened an old knife!

4/6/07

<u>HOME</u>

Back home today, good bye jail
A little thinner, somewhat pale
Designer notes on my door
Home, couldn't ask for more

A friend I can honestly trust
Agree loyalty is a must
His daughter reached beyond her fears
Filled my cold empty eyes with tears

A second family that feels real
Emotional wounds may begin to heal
Learning once again to smile
They've been absent for awhile

I really felt at home today
Thank you both for allowing me to stay
Another brother and a niece
Tonight my soul may rest in peace

Dedicated to Jay and Erica
4/17/07

LOSING HOPE

No hopes, no dreams and back to jail?
Is this how Christ felt waiting for the last nail?
Hung as an example for all to see
Has life finally defeated me?

Throughout time, the opinions of me have been mixed
After twelve years Alyse believes I can't be fixed
Mother said her strength has been washed away by tears
Because dying before my release is a constant fear

Tommy simply made the statement "You've got to change"
Yet I believe at this point happiness is beyond range
Badge and Pooky are full of love and concern
Could this be big brothers final crash and burn?

My soul could be used as a display model
Showing the effects of life at full throttle
A heart so broken and no longer red
Making my emotions the casualties left for dead

4/22/07

PREPARATION

I write you this poem as time begins to fade
Looks like prison another price to be paid
Not looking for you to say it'll be alright
Wanting you to hug me with all your might

One touching memory to decorate my cell
A security blanket to sleep with in Hell
Something to bring back a smile
Strengthen me for my next trial

Please quit kicking me when I'm down
I blame only myself for the fools' crown
Don't want it to become too late
Can't hug you through a prison gate

If you must hear me say again you're right
Then as a fool I bow out of this fight
Something I'll never understand
Why must I receive your fist and not your tender hand?

Dedicated to Nikki
5/10/07

HEAD STONE

Hidden in the cold emptiness of my eyes
Emotions damaged by a life full of lies
Keep searching and you'll find what remains of a heart
Once filled with love and dreams, through time, was torn apart

Don't be afraid to ask how or why?
Yes I can be dead without having to die
When the love and emotion in my soul was bled
My mind and body joined the rest of the living dead

Awakened some nights by a tear running down my face
In a world that becomes a dark and lonely place
There is no greater fear than feeling absolutely alone
The tear was to remind me the fault is my own

Can't remember the last gentle words whispered into my ear
I will admit that loneliness is my greatest fear
Punishment, I believe, for my evil doing is to be alone
Finally, the word loneliness cut into my headstone!

3/4/08

LISTEN FRIEND

After the sun has risen
Ending your first night in prison
Wishing you would've stopped to listen
Too late now, the whole world is missing

To busy and no time to talk
Alone in the prison yard as you walk
Last night's tears left your eyes blood red
Forced out by thoughts of home gathering in your head

Never looking for a reason to stop
Focused only on the path to the top
Then arrives your first visiting day
Your reason has come to see her father locked away

Times up and now return to your cell
Preparing for another night in hell
Watching your child trying to be strong
The question is for how long!

8/08

HIGHWAYMEN

STANDING TALL AND DRESSED IN BLACK
DISPLAYING THE EMBLEM ON HIS BACK
ONLY HE KNOWS WHERE HE'S BEEN
LIVING LIFE AS A DETROIT HIGHWAYMEN

GLADIATORS ON WHEELS THE PEOPLE SAY
TAKING CARE OF BUSINESS, NO TIME TO PLAY
ON STEEL HORSES WE WILL ARRIVE
TWO BY TWO AND VERY MUCH ALIVE

BUILT ON BLOOD, SWEAT, AND TEARS
A FAMILY FOR MORE THAN FIFTY YEARS
IN YOUR MIND LET THERE BE NO DOUBT
PRIDE IS WHAT THE DETROIT HIGHWAYMEN ARE ALL
ABOUT!

PRISON CITY CREW

12/08

A LESSON

Will you stop and listen, I've been there
You're just way too busy to care
Listening to only yourself talk
Be prepared for a very long walk

Ideas about friendship change with age
Mine were shaped by five years in a cage
Never taking a few moments to stop and listen
Awake one day with all my friends missin'

Sadly the best lessons, are the ones we're forced to learn
Arriving shortly after the emotional crash and burn
We then reach out to those we left behind
Not even memories are we able to find

Soul emptied as I passed the first prison gate
Overwhelmed by regrets and knowing it's too late
Now with so many bridges and fences to mend
Do we finally take that moment to define friend

12/05/08

A TRAP

Awoke this morning a little more broken than yesterday
The weight of the world mounting in a painful way
Bodies become weak and age blankets ambition
Heart and mind blame one another for our soul's poor condition

Ran through life strong and full of life
Only to find the devil has taken the world's side
As we stumble through each day of the year
Thoughts become entangled wondering why we're here

Suddenly we're offered freedoms dangling from above
Braided so tight and greased with Satan's love
With an evil grin, he dangles his nylon gift
Knowing when the kicking stops, the soul is left to drift

When you feel the load is impossible to bare
Simply remember those surrounding you and that they care
Remind yourself that we get one life and no second shot
Farewell to the cowards caught in the devil's slip knot

4/02/09

DEMONS TALKING

Game over? Must be finished with me
What remains you left tied to the whipping tree
Warned once about how you play
Picking away at emotions day after day

Someone must've forgotten to enlighten you
Emotional anger can make any man a fool
I also have a game I enjoy playing
Only at the end with emotions you'll be playing

Yes I have demons that are hard to restrain
All of which enjoy administering pain
They've become specialists at verbal abuse
I feel them scratching inside, wanting to be loose

For years at a time they're locked in a cage
Until someone arrives to fill them with rage
Teasing them with lies made of words of hope
Whipping them with an emotional rope

Outside in the world, not much do I fear
I'm afraid of what's locked inside and the voices I hear
Awakened by cynical laughter
Stolen emotions are what my demons will be after!

4/02/09

THINKING OF YOU

It's so very hard to explain
That your absence causes me pain
Daily I think of your smile
Separated by just over a mile

Damn this world that divided our joy
My love for you cannot be destroyed
I still spend time wishing to be together
Becoming soul mates from now thru forever

Always seeing things from a different light
Guilty of letting stubbornness blur my sight
Tongues as sharp as razors often cutting to the bone
Never knowing when to leave well enough alone

Tears still try to wash memories away
Hidden deep beyond the heart most will stay
In the silence of the night I pay the price
Remembering that lying next to you felt so nice

More than once I've said a prayer
Asking God to take me back there
Wondering what it might take
To prove our love was never a mistake

My pain to others I refuse to reveal
It's become dessert at every lonely meal
The world should know one thing for certain
I will love you until it draws the final curtain

Dedicated to Nikki
4/08/09

WILD CHILD

Taken by surprise in an unlikely place
She was dressed in leather not satin or lace
Keeping my emotions at a safe distance
Mind and heart argued over the amount of resistance

Reminded of a life full of secrets and dead ends
No belief in God or trust in many friends
My moon filled with loneliness each and every night
Happiness so far away and always out of sight

Few have been the moment filled with peace and joy
When my heart would allow itself to become a toy
Though years of pain I've built up my defenses
Draining my emotions to cover the expenses

In those times of feeling misunderstood
I almost forgot that some people can be good
With the soft touch of your hand you'd wipe away fears
I could then enjoy the soft words placed into my ears

If for some unseen reason tomorrow it should all end
I believe I will always be able to call you friend
Remembering that in your arms I peacefully slept
I trust, with you, my secret will be kept

Dedicated to Nikki
8/12/09

GIORGI

Sound the alert, Hell is about to start
Evil has shed her skin in search of a heart
Once disguised as honesty, speaking words of trust
Manipulating fools with lies and lust

Sinking fangs into the soul creating imperfections
Smiling as she sends friends in opposite directions
No regrets about how any soul may feel
Laughing as she sits to smoke her next meal

Making you believe she's better than the rest
Lacking a heart beneath her dark nippled breasts

Using her sparkling eyes to keep blame misdirected
Touching you so her venom can be injected

Proclaiming to all, she's not that kind of girl
Still collecting necklaces, all made of pearl
Telling you the rumors are all lies
Hated by girls but spoiled by drugs every man buys

It would serve you right for the damage you've done
If some other person started having fun
In no way or form is this a threat
Your star will soon shine, thanks to the internet

8/16/09

LOYALTY

Through life it's been safer to travel alone
Although loneliness often cuts to the bone
Failure becomes the sparkle in jealous eyes
Loyalty costumes our enemy's lies

Voices from every direction shout "I got your back"
In reality, you never know whose loyalty you lack
Stepping forward trying not to be scared
Hoping in failure, pride can be spared

Finally it has become my turn
Another opportunity with lessons to learn
For it is not failure we should fear, but
Allowing things to move too fast, we can't steer

If into the eyes of failure I must stare
With lessons, we've learned, I'll arrive there
Throughout life I've gambled with pride
Double my bet, tell the dealer, "I let it ride".

12/3/09

FORTY-SEVEN

How did I ever make it to forty-seven?
One thing is for certain, no dreams of heaven
I have no one to blame for my path through life
Searching for shortcuts with a gun and knife

Let me say to those people I've called friend
I believe in loyalty until the bitter end
Forming my own opinion, who cares what people say
Those cowards spreading rumors someday will pay

For mistakes, big prices I have paid
I refuse to compromise any friendship I've made
With a handful of those closer than brothers
Always careful to protect their identity from others

It's too bad all people can't think the same
Friendship was never meant to be a game
If you are one who allows the game to begin
Blame only yourself if it ends with a SIN

1/26/10

IN THE MORNING

Sitting with my mind tangled in thought
About things I'm sure can't be bought
Like those precious moments in your arms before facing the day
So intoxicating they almost force me to stay

Priceless is the tone of your voice saying "I Love You"
With a smile I turn and say "I know you do"
Your back to sleep before I close the door
Wishing I didn't have to work anymore

Throughout the day you dance in my head
A little memory of you tucked in bed
Pillows, blankets, and one lazy dog
Stretched out beside you like a hairy log

Time just doesn't move fast enough
Without you every day is lonely and rough
Thoughts return to something you said
"Hurry home babe, I'll be waiting in bed"

At that very moment the alarm begins ringing
Not to mention, the damn birds begins singing
Once again awakened from a perfect dream
Dog barking, me yelling, and you with that dreadful morning
scream!

Dedicated to Nikki
2/2/10

FUN

Can you believe it all started as fun?
Just wanting to fit in with everyone
We began to avoid the nostril burn
Smoking off foil was the best thing to learn

Ignoring the warnings about the beast
How he'd grab you when you expected it least
Helping you form excuses as you became distant
Unable to function without your new assistant

Then you notice the stranger in your mirror
An empty face and eyes full of fear
Emotions lost at the side of the road
Refusing to believe anything we're told

Everyone is lying and we're doing just fine
Filling our foil line after line
Then all at once we're standing alone
Cold and calloused with a heart made of stone

How did it get so far out of hand?
Adrift in the ocean with no sight of land
Believing once we had everything under control
Gave birth to an emotional zombie with an empty soul.

2/13/10

THE RETURN

Don't cry to me about your emptiness
It's only because you forgot your dealers address
Can't fill the void where once was a heart
Told you someday your world would fall apart

Warned you that the beast would get his grip
That you couldn't afford the price of that trip
Well, well look at you now, so alone and lost
Did your house, children, and job cover the cost?

Yes, that's right, I'm gonna turn my back
You and the beast stole any emotions I lack
It's no longer my job to make the tears stop
Isn't that what you said when I fell from the top?

What happened, I thought you knew it all?
I see you've learned something new - how to crawl
Don't be mistaken I won't offer my hand
Laughing while I watch you sit, bark and stand

Late again, offered my arm years ago
Remember you laughed and of the beast wouldn't let go
I'll just enjoy all of your tears as I stand and stare
Because when I reached for you, you weren't even there!

2/15/10

<u>GOVERNMENT LIES</u>

The rumbling of the motors was stopped
To listen for whose names had been dropped
Where have they gone, all those men dressed in black
Those who once rode proud and strong in the pack

Loyalty now infected after being impaled
Has placed some in coffins with lids to be nailed
To the enemy do not surrender your last breath
There's no such thing as life after death

What would the fathers of our reputation say?
If they could witness brotherhood being thrown away
With a solid oath of loyalty this journey begins
Promising in blood to never reveal any brothers sins

The government has labeled us as organized thugs
With allegations that include murder and drugs
Leading the public to believe we should be incarcerated
Allows for a smoke screen while civil rights are violated

To the public and brothers who willingly submit
We salute you with a mouth full of spit
Allow us to pray for your spineless snitching souls
Hoping that you'll be buried in shit filled holes!!

2/23/10

<u>CHECKED OUT</u>

You introduce yourself to each day
Hoping no one knows you've gone away
That your mind has simply checked out
A major violation of what sanity is about

Under weight of an abused conscience
The brain adopts rules of no nonsense
Separating memories into fact or fiction
Sometimes revealing a painful addiction

Allowing no one to see you cry
Passing the day with a smile that's a lie
To yourself, you must be true
For happiness to work for you

If it's still impossible to retrieve
Does the problem lie in what you believe?
Could it be an evil heart?
Denying happiness a brand new start

To heal a soul with such a division
Forces the brain to make a decision
Wide open in search of God, or
Race toward the flame at Satan's nod!

3/2/10

REGRETFUL MEMORY

Last night as I watched you sleep
I felt emotions that were hidden so deep
On your face your thoughts could be seen
Damn, you were looking forward to April fifteen

Hating what I've become as I face prison
Clearly has caused you to make a decision
Listen as I apologize for hurting you in any way
Smile - freedom is closer with each passing day

The thought I had as I kissed your forehead
I bet she's dreaming of filling me with lead
So much has changed since we started out
Have we decided to forget what respect is about?

In a moment you pulled up the covers
What happened to the days when we were lovers?
Wishing I could truly express how I feel inside
Touching you in anger caused my soul to die

Dedicated to Nikki
4/19/10

IN MEMORY OF SHAYLA

I watch my friend cry today
The love of his life has been taken away
Step back with your biblical reasons
We're not talking about the changing seasons

She'll never return to whisper in his ear
No messages left on the bathroom mirror
Nineteen years spent finding her spot on earth
Grasping at hope and love, what was that worth?

Hang them all by their necks for this sin
Let them swing in their newly stretched skin
Slaughter their souls for Satan's feast
It was a young girl they killed, not a rabid beast

Who cared if the bible says "it's better to forgive"
Where the hell was God when she whispered "I want to live"?
I say burn the pages of his holy book
Introduce all eight to the slaughtering hook

Dedicated to my friend
"She may never come back, but she'll always have your back"
8/8/10

KNOCK KNOCK

No, no don't answer that door
Yes you've heard that knock before
It's the beast with his seductive grin
With smiles and laughter he works his way in

Inviting you to inhale him through your nose
Inside, slowly, your addiction grows
Then you try him off a smooth piece of foil
The addiction causes your blood to boil

Forward to the needle, blast him into a vein
Not feeding the addiction, now causes you pain
For every problem you'll begin to welcome him
Worked out nicely for my friends Tia and Jim

Another friend answered the door
Now he craves more, more, more
Often seen in three day clothes
He dropped forty pounds as his zombie arose

The beast also hides behind my temper without a sound
Only to explode one night and beat you down
If you answer that door thinking you're better than us
We'll save you a seat on the hell-bound bus

Full of victims taken with that seductive grin
Only to hear Satan ask "where have you been?"

11/19/10

SHADOWED FACES

Awakened by an awful dream
Sweat flowing like a swollen stream
Being watched by shadowed faces
Hands tied with leather laces

Their eyes burn through my soul
Torturing me seems their only goal
Night after night they return
Life as I know it continues to burn

I was told once to use love as a shield
Still the shadowed faces refuse to yield
Dreams continue to pick up speed
On my soul demons continue to feed

They showed no respect when they were alive
What will they do if once again I arrive?
Haunting me with memories must be their plan
Since both became memories because of a man

I welcome them into my tortured soul
With my blood, flesh, and spirit fill your bowl
Just when you believe you can enjoy your feast
Your final memories, will be the words of a Priest!

12/10/10

HATE

Let me tell you about the birthplace of hate
It lies well beyond the fires at hells gate
Hidden deep beneath Satan's burning throne
It will consume mind, body, and every last bone

First it causes thoughts to spiral into an abyss
Demons begin rejoicing, drinking bottles of Satan's piss
Waiting for your mind to let them in
At that moment the infection will begin

Demons chain your soul to the whipping post
Where hate is allowed to feed on its newest host
Feeling the infection move through each stage
Now tied to the whipping post creature full of rage

If you happen to break free
You're someone no one wants to see
No one knows exactly how you feel
Because hate offers everyone a different deal!

12/10/10

GUILT

Guilt through the ages has driven men mad
It can convince us that what feels good is bad
With the power to change any personality
Sometimes acting like an express lane to reality

Guilt has led some to believe it would be better to die
Becoming their only reason for telling the world good bye
Ultimately guilt points us in the direction of honesty
This only happens if the mind and heart manage to agree

Guilt is tied to both wrong and right
Causing the mind and emotions to constantly fight
Depending on which of the two finally wins
Decides whether or not we live with our sins

Guilt through the ages has driven men mad
Because they weren't satisfied with what they had
Do the best you can with what you've got
That will keep your mind and heart in the right spot

12/11/10

WORKING

Quiet, did you hear that sound?
Look out the window, anyone around?
All is clear, work can begin
Lock all the doors and let no one in

Staying at home to create your newest friend
One that so many hold onto until the end
It's not dinner that's just been cooked
But a hunger that will keep you hooked

Pushing two or three days into one
Until your body announced it's done
Still refusing to sleep, you reach for your meds
The ones declared illegal by the feds

So easy to make that anyone can learn
Tell that to those who have suffered a burn
Your skin peels back and blisters bust open
To avoid infection is what they were hoping

If you believe above all this you have risen
Soon you'll receive a prize: an all-expense paid trip to prison
So when you get busted trying to get rich
Be found with your mouth shut and not in some ditch!

12/12/10

FORCED TO THE FLAME

The phone rang late one January night
"Chacho come quick, things didn't go right.
Bring bandages, cream and something for the pain
Oh my God, all of this is insane"

Arriving as fast as I could
No hospital, by all, was well understood
She worked in silence with no mention of blame
Trying to repair the damage done by the flame

Burnt chest and face with eyes swollen shut
I stood silent with a knot in my gut
The room had filled with the stench of burnt skin
I believe his wife prayed that infection wouldn't set in

Trying to make money to avoid going to jail
With no job, the bills were piling up in the mail
The courts don't care about anyone's story
Well fuck them and fill their ass with ole glory

In time when all is said and done
I don't believe anyone would say it was really fun
Everyday most people struggle to survive
Some become like me, dead, only pretending to be alive!!!

1/13/11

BAD NEWS

Have you heard the news today?
Someone special has been taken away
Leaving my friend with a broken heart
In moments his world fell apart

Memories also begin to flood the mind
Fact and fiction forever entwined
Hidden are the answers to the question, "Why"
Confused and alone my friend could only cry

To you people who believe in the man upstairs
What the fuck does it take before he cares?
Did you decide my friend couldn't pass your test?
So you took away what he enjoyed best

I think it's time for you to quit cheating
Prepare a special place for the daughter you'll be meeting
Maybe next time you can show you care
Just do more than sit and stare

3/28/11

TOUGH

I can't believe how tough you are
Tougher than most men, by far
Anything they can do, you can do better
What about the woman inside?, Oh ya, forget her

You can smoke, drink, swear, and ride
All that helps the real you hide
Always very careful to not shed a tear
Wouldn't want the other men thinking you're queer

They've taught you it's a must to be in control
Advice given while riding, drinking, and smoking a bowl
Trying so hard to get your mind perfectly impaired
Making it so much easier to say you never cared

I hope some night while you're lying alone
You'll be surprised that you don't have a bone
Wish I could see the tears roll down your face
When you find, like most men, being tough is a lonely place!

Dedicated to a friend I thought really cared
9/8/11

<u>HYPOCRITE</u>

Damn, I've never seen anyone so good
At turning off emotions like I wish I could
You believe love is only a word
Having no value, no matter how often heard

Believing all questions should be answered with "WHY"
Yet always able to justify a good lie
Always knowing exactly what to say
The foundation for always getting your way

A master at getting someone to believe
Those who don't, well, you simply deceive
If by some chance you ever get caught
You sell the same lie until it is bought

Above all this what I think is best
Is how you declare you're not like the rest?
You're right, everyone can see she is a whore
Perhaps no one taught her to first close the door!

9/8/11

FROM A FRIEND

Does anyone see your soul?
Does anyone see your pain?
It seems that they are all out for what they have to gain
The secrets that you have to keep, the torment that you hide
Will only give you move nightmares and eat you up inside
You wonder how you've made it this far.
You wonder why you're alive.
I'll tell you my friend, you have so much to give.
The power to change people's lives
You must learn to forgive, you've tormented
yourself enough. It's okay to cry, you don't
have to be so tough.
Just remember that you have value, and
People who do love you.
Perhaps you'll find comfort in these words
and they help you make it through

9/19/11

SOME FORM OF APOLOGY

The cold breeze of loneliness has created a chill
Through a broken heart that love use to fill
It takes a simple tear to roll down my face
Reminding me once again, I've fallen from grace

Caught by surprise by how fast you can run
Does it help by forgetting any good I've ever done?
I'm no angel and I've lead an evil life
Never have I been so injured by a verbal knife

Carving slowly at any sense of pride
Even demons stop once the victims cried
You enjoy kicking them when they're down
Until on their own salty tears they drown

Our emotions have been spilt all over the ground
Respect for one another is nowhere to be found
Both so guilty of hurting one another
Yet only one is willing to give up on the other

I wish I could had you all of the blame
Playing with fire got me burnt by the flame
Yes I'll take the blame for your emotional wreck
Started with wrapping my hands around your neck

Sorry is never the answer to why
The cure for crying is never a lie
Life seems like a battle when happiness we seek
Truth and love always seem so weak

Do you remember how we use to smile?
People could hear us laughing for at least a mile
How things have changed since way back then
Thoughts are now about Who, What, Where and When.

10/30/11

THE LETTER

I watched a man open his mail today
Never seen anyone weep in such a way
He'd been left by his girl after promising she'd wait
No real explanation for moving out of state

He looked up at me with a tear in each eye
Asking me softly "Why did she lie?"
Not waiting for an answer he continued to read
I told him beware of sorrow, the sharks will feed

Without another word, he tucked the letter in his shirt
His way of saving his heart from anymore hurt
Covered himself with his blanket to drift off to sleep
Never thought a man could feel pain so deep

To hold back my own tears took all my might
My first prayer in years was for him that night
It wasn't until the next morning that I cried
When the guard said "In his sleep, the man had died"

11/16/11

DINNER

O.K. it's count time, back to the cell
All goes quiet as we listen for the dinner bell
In single file we all head to chow
The guards pull you out of line. What the fuck now!

Arms out from your sides while being shook-down
Front all checked, now slowly turn around
What are they looking for? Who really knows
Sure is fucking cold out here, bet it snows

O.K. move along. You've been cleared
Meatloaf and peas, just what I feared
Eat as fast as you can and try not to chew
With no choices what else can I do?

Single file as we head back to the dorm
Those few early snowflakes have become a storm
Damn, again pulled out of line to be checked
Fuck, can't blame anyone for the life I wrecked!

11/16/11

VISITING DAY

Was that my name they just called for a visit?
Walking from barrack to control wondering "who is it?"
Wondering what all I was going to say
Damn, today turned out to be a wonderful day

Would I be looking into my girls eyes?
Or answering a list of my mother's whys?
Didn't really matter, someone was here
Being forgotten is an inmate's biggest fear

Could it be my younger brother?
Scrambled my brain, couldn't think of another
I guess it doesn't matter when you're in this place
Glad this morning, I decided to shave my face

Stepped into control all ready for my visit
Still totally confused on who it is or isn't
With emotions and nerves all wrapped in a ball
The guard says "It wasn't your name we meant to call"

11/17/11

ANOTHER ONE SLIPS AWAY

Well, let another one slip away, number forty-eight
Damn, only two doors down from fifty's gate
Where have they gone? What have I done?
Wish I could say they've all been fun

Rushed through childhood way to fast
Allowing my future to be infected by the past
Wrestling throughout my teen years made mom proud
That was her son being cheered on by the crowd

Graduation day then on to college
Trying to arm myself with culture and knowledge
Here was my shot at setting my own rules
Like so many others, followed a path full of fools

Living my own life, got lost on the street
Must've fell asleep while sitting in the driver seat
Judge said "wake up, your sentenced to five years in prison"
After all these years no higher have I risen

11/23/11

WOUNDED

Trying to walk away from the words trapped in my head.
Your voice shouts "I hate you liar and I wish you were dead".
Too bad you aren't here. I think your wish is coming true.
Heart broken and a soul that's dying…what do I do?

Never thought pain could be felt so deep.
A broken heart is a secret men should keep.
How do I keep the tears from falling from my eyes?
Can't explain how I feel, tongue tangled up with lies.

Like fighting an addiction, the pain eats me from inside.
Emotions become entangled then struggles with my pride.
Can't deny that fear has gathered in my eyes.
A soul will never heal if bandaged up with lies.

Should've listened to the warnings that it would arrive.
When a dead man walking in couldn't pretend to be alive,
Revealing a soul empty and now all alone
Announcing the truth to the world…the blame is MY OWN!

2012

FEELING YOU

I FEEL YOU UNDER MY SKIN

AN ADDICTION IN THE MAKING

I FEEL YOU FLOWING THROUGH VEINS

AN ADDICTION IN THE MAKING

I FEEL MY HEART WITH THOUGHTS OF YOU

AN ADDICTION IN THE MAKING

I FEEL THE WORDS I LOVE YOU ON MY LIPS

THE ADDICTION HAS BEEN CREATED!

1/9/12

DRIVING ME *INSANE*

Damn it, can't run anymore
I think you're faster than before
Is it the chase that makes you smile
Or the fact that you're the queen of denial

Feeding me loneliness of every flavor
Helps you forget any of my good behavior
Speaking of the future and sins I'll commit
Into your plans, I'm sure you'll make them fit

Preaching that honesty is always best
Honestly, did you ever pass that test?
Must've been before you became a professor of pain
Specializing in driving men insane

Studying the best methods for making men shed tears
And their role in manipulating their fears
Even if that includes the use of lies
All the while, looking right into their eyes

Guilt is also used while cultivating the art
Some women believe it's the most intricate part
Sparking sporadic attempts at forgiveness
Only to be rewarded with more loneliness

1/11/2012

MY TURN

Vengeance is mine, I want you to feel my pain
Asking me between breaths" have I gone insane?"
The cost of my broken heart, with your life would be paid
I loved you once, then with my emotions you played

If it were left up to me, I'd simply dig a hole
To bury you alive with every emotion that you stole
I promise a tear in every shovel full of dirt
As your screaming fades away, so will my hurt

How could I ever forgot all you've done
So when it's possible, I'll dig you up for fun
That way your bones can feel the summer air
Allowing the animals to pick them bare

Finally when they've been bleached totally white
I will place them in a sack to be buried right
Over in the shade of the old maple tree
You know the one, where the neighborhood dogs come to pee

1/24/12

I'M SORRY

Wish I had an "I'm sorry" that could heal all your sorrow
Then all the pain of today could disappear by tomorrow
It would also wipe away all those senseless tears
Giving you back your happiness, taken by your fears

Wish I had an "I'm sorry" for every telling you a lie
So you would never have a memory that might ever make you
cry
Allowing every word spoken to you to be delivered by a smile
Followed by a laughter that could be heard for a mile

Wish I had an "I'm sorry" that was worth more than a dime
So the years you spent with me, wouldn't feel like wasted time
I know the only "I'm sorry" I have will be met by hate
No longer having value and is arriving way too late!

I expect you won't believe these words but if ever my "I'm
sorry" can equal
Your forgiveness, I hope "I'm sorry" never again will be used.

1/24/12

SOUNDS & SIGNS

A rooster craves announcing a new day.
Twenty-four more hours of feeling this way.
Standing alone feeling so sorry and sad.
Guilty again of treating love so bad.

Listening as the wind blows through every leafless tree
Brings an early loneliness to the emptiness inside of me.
Mind and body now argue about what's best for my soul.
How to heal the wound that left a deep dark hole.

Silently a raven collects trinkets that shine,
Creating a vision of you with a heart once mine.
Prize well secured she flies off to her nest.
The possession of my heart sets you apart from the rest.

The afternoon breeze carries a lonely dogs bark;
Clouds gather trying to make the day dark.
A smile returns to my face as memories of you play
Bringing some warmth to my solitary autumn day.

Friends then arrive saying everything will be alright.
Easy for them to say…they're not sleeping alone tonight.
Loneliness forever my greatest fear.
Until your voice once again whispers in my ear.

2/5/12

FOR DANI

I can hear you throughout each passing day
Asking "Where did my life go so astray?"
Looking back at all the things you've done
Asking "God Damn is this all I've won?"

Out own our own believing happiness only money could buy
Asking "who was it that first told you that lie?"
Finally, it just fucking hurts to look back
Asking "what do I do to get back on track?"

Direct your thoughts to the future and smile.
Then dedicate yourself, travel that miracle mile.
You might find victims who have lost their race,
I'll tell you my theory, the secrets all in the pace.

You'll have days when you just want to quit.
Your soul will tell your body "Fuck it. Let's sit".
Soul isn't the boss; the brain runs it all.
Its decisions keep soul and pride standing tall.

Study each decision that runs throughout your mind.
Make the next race one you don't have to run blind.
Life for you hasn't stopped; it's placed on a shelf
To be returned when once again you believe in yourself.

Never focus on the finish, first find the starting line.
Eyes now wide open, read every warning sign.
Surround yourself with lessons learned inside.
Start with the one that reminds us that life is not a free ride!

Dedicated to my friend Dani
7/24/12

<u>KICKING PRIZE</u>

A razor tongue has sliced away my soul
Allowing you to pace into a grave the heart you stole.
Black clouds have kidnapped the mighty son.
Life as I knew it was over, gone and done.

Though I didn't say I want to hold you so tight,
Rejection simply dimmed loves guiding light.
Truly lost the entire time you were gone,
Hoping you were missing me, only to be wrong.

With money, faith, and trust now all spent
Concern, compassion, and love to hell all been sent.
It's said that love and happiness can't be bought,
Is that the reason manipulation and acting are taught?

"I HATE YOU" you've shouted placing a noose over my neck,
Laughter fills your soul as you give the rope its final check.
Are your hands prepared to release the rope they're grasping?
Then your ears will capture the sounds of a man gasping.

Finally when the kicking stops and legs are covered with piss,
Satan will cut down his prize, thinking you with a kiss.
Let me inform you this time he will be disappointed,
For I am the evil with which the demons are anointed.

A new deck of cards will be cut and fairly dealt,
Will this hand make you feel what your victims all have felt?
Will it answer the question "what's behind my evil grin?"
It is really a soul filled with vindictiveness and sin?

8/10/12

BLAME

We allow no one passage to our mind,
No witnesses to thoughts running blind
Mental graffiti that won't leave us alone.

The work of artists unknown.
Their contributions have shaped our belief,
That for a broker heart there is no relief.
We find it cheaper to pay rent on loneliness,
Than the price of owning the idea of happiness.

It's been said to walk we must first crawl.
Only after we've become brave enough to fall
We must learn there is no shame in falling down.

Since reality, for most, is found closest to the ground
We'd like to believe we always will know what's in store.
Driven by fears of what's happened before.
Pointing our fingers at one another for being apart.
Could it be that nether is actually brave enough to start?!?!?

9/10/12

JUST A LITTLE "THANK-YOU" POEM

You tried to keep me comfortable each night.
I'd fall asleep with you holding my hand so tight.
You always knew when I was lying about my pain.
Off you'd go to find someone to explain.

Sensing a build-up in my frustration,
You'd shine light on the situation.
I enjoyed working on your smile.
Your pressure pushed me every inch of the mile.

I could never explain what your support mean.
At my side so much of your time was spent.
Next to me because you wanted to stay.
So I say "thank you" for loving in your own way.

Dedicated to Nikki
10/18/12

IN A CHAIR

Let me take a moment to tell you of a friend,
Who five years ago almost met his bitter end.
A brutal accident placed him in a wheelchair.
Reality is that life doesn't always play so fair.

Quietly, I'm sure, there are days he wishes he would've died.
Those days are pushed aside with the arrival of his pride.
People take for granted the fact that we can stand.
Humbling is the struggle to move his finger on each hand.

Refusing to be limited by things he cannot do,
Makes each and every day a struggle to get through.
Welcome are the memories of days that were much more fun.
Sometimes that's all he has to clear clouds from the sun.

Friends offer him their help, doing what they can,
Careful to remember my friend is still a man.
Once over six feet tall surviving on his own,
Now it is a victory to simply answer his ringing phone.

People should learn to laugh that their life ain't so sad
Until you lose it all and every movement hurts so bad.
My friend wakes every morning ready for a fight
Then bravely faces every obstacle – morning, noon, and night.

12/30/12

<u>HAUNTED</u>

Sitting in the glow of the television
Haunted by a never ending vision
Calloused hands wipe away the tears
Hands that once fought off all my fears.

Broken and bent from a lifetime at war
Now struggle to simply open a door.
Against memories they are of no use.
Defenseless against an emotional noose.

They held you softly with the strength of a bear,
To become the reasons you're no longer there.
Made you a promise my hands would later break,
Wish I could've known the cost of that mistake.

Unleashed my hands on a destructive path,
Your body fell victim to their mindless wrath
Causing us both unforgiveable pain;
Yours physical and mine in the brain.

Sitting in the glow of the television
Haunted still by that dreadful decision
Calloused hands wipe away a stream
Filled with tears and an escaping dream!

Dedicated to Nikki
1/3/13

<u>SENTENCED</u>

I don't need whiskey to drown out the pain;
I'll hide my tears in the pouring rain.
With no attorneys to plead my case;
Found guilty with a slap across the face.

Serving time for crimes against your heart,
Regret builds up every day we're apart.
I'm filled with emotions on visiting day,
Only to feel so empty when you walk away.

Unable to snap the chains of solitude
Renders loneliness the dominate mood.
For a lifetime by greatest fear,
Now it surrounds me in every mirror.

My words golden once upon a time.
"I love you" and "sorry" now have the value of a dime.
Can't even afford to ask you to listen,
Called a liar when I say "it's you I'm missin'".

If the day ever arrives that I'm set free
Will it be you that's there waiting for me?
I'll rebuild every bridge I've every burned
Using the lessons I've been forced to learn.

1/15/13

FOR MOM

In a moment you were lying on the ground.
The world went quiet, your pain the only sound.
Your sons rushed from every direction
To help, hold, and comfort you with their affection.

Your tear brought on memories with a blast
Of long fearful nights we endured in the past.
Now as then, you wouldn't stay down.
Wiping your tears, in tears you wouldn't drown.

Feeling your pain as the ambulance drove away,
At your side four sons vowed to stay.
Lying there in pain, mom, who taught us to survive
To be men when days like this arrive.

You told us not to worry and that you'd be alright.
Suddenly the clouds cleared and the sun was shining bright.
The lesson may have been that time will take its toll,
Yet even time won't remove you from our soul.

1/16/13

SLEEPING WITH A MEMORY

Sleeping with a memory since you decided to part
Can't stop the bleeding from my broken heart.
You said "I love you, can't believe you lied"
Today my soul took its final breath and died.

Your smile was a beautiful sight to see.
It is karma that keeps it so far from me?
When alone, I softly whisper your name
Apologizing for any tears and accepting blame.

My mind can't forget you, my heart needs your touch.
Without you beside me the pain has become too much.
I know when my tears all stop falling
Once again the demons inside will come calling.

Somehow you kept everything together.
By myself life is filed with stormy weather.
If there is a God in heaven, hear my prayer.
Tell her I love her, she's out there somewhere.

1/22/13

<u>GOT PLAYED</u>

Disappeared with my heart and smile,
Surprised at your cowardly style.
Now refusing to respond in any way
Thinking I'll forget with each passing day.

If pain is what you wanted me to feel,
Hit the bullseye making my heart your meal.
Laughing because you left me an empty plate,
I used it for dessert, an order of hate.

You make it look so simple and easy to forget.
Let me remind you…it's far from over yet.
You are the only thing occupying my mind.
Sorry if you don't like what you find.

Your mistake was to under estimate this man.
I have also developed a master plan.
Played for a fool from the very start,
Confirmed when I trusted you with my heart.

In the spring the city will come alive.
Is there room for both of us to survive?
Remember my heart and how it was done.
Honestly, there won't be room under the sun!

1/23/13

SOMETHING OTHER THAN HATE

Can't believe it ended with a lie,
Afraid to look me in the eye.
I'd like to write of my hate,
That I think of you as demon bait.

I know well what they're capable of,
Specializing in hate, feeding on love
Reminding me that your gift was pain.
Their venom flows through each vein.

Good idea to hide like a coward.
Daily my demons become empowered.
The voices in my head scream retribution.
Do unto others as done to – a demon solution.

Multiplying with each passing day,
Becoming harder to keep them at bay.
If any escape – well – know I tried.
Mark that as the date my soul died.

It all doesn't excite me anymore.
Afraid for you if I can't hold the door.
Oh why did you end it this way?
Demons begging: Nikki come play!

1/26/13

FIRST KISS LIED

Over for years and a million miles ago,
We met laughing, little did we know.
Your pretty eyes doored me with danger
As if to ask: Are you brave enough stranger?

I couldn't close my eyes, turn or run.
At that moment my heart was done.
Our first kiss told us both a lie.
It said that we'd never make each other cry.

Tears now fall, looking at where we are now.
Neither of us know who, what, where, when or how.
With our worlds almost out of sight
I grasp the memory of us being together day and night.

Once I could hold you so tight every day,
Somehow I let it all just slip away.
I'm so sorry that I ever made you cry
That caused your love for me to die.

1/30/13

POETRY

My poetry speaks for people not often heard.
It gives trapped emotions the freedom of a bird.
Emotions that seem tangled become easy to understand.
The value of expression puts the world in hand.

When a poem seems to have a familiar plot
It's our mind that give it life or not.
Poetry can form a bridge to love or span the tragic.
Interpretation is what gives poetry its magic.

A poem that makes some people feel sad
Might open the eyes of some who've been bad.
It all depends on the tone of the readers' voice.
That could suddenly open a new avenue of choice.

Poetry is a key that could open so many doors;
An opportunity for all – from kings to whores.
Allow the verses to make you their guest.
Your interpretation is as valuable as the rest.

1/30/13

THE STORE

Casualties pile up like never before.
Across the street the neighborhood store.
People, in and out, throughout the night.
Hours kept with a porch light.

The special of the day – homemade – try it.
People come from everywhere just to buy it.
No one cares with what it is made,
They're more concerned about how much they paid.

An explosion, headlines in the evening news.
One person dies, burnt from head to shoes.
Another store opens as another's door close.
All it takes is plastic bottles and some rubber hose.

The chase for the dollar sign in their eyes,
Opens the door to a world shaped by lies.
One that doesn't really care who's dead,
Where the souls of the living are bled.

Casualties pile up like never before.
Tomorrow will the pile start outside your door?
Will it be your mother that cries?
Losing her child to a world shaped by lies.

2/1/13

EXECUTIVE ADVICE

Since you feel like becoming the man,
How about filling all of us in on the plan.
First priority is the picking of a crew,
Not chasing young bitches to possibly screw.

Their loyalty ends, if you can't meet their demands.
Off to chase the wallet in another man's hands.
Your crew should make people respect your voice.
Picking tested men would be the very best choice.

Of course the final choice is totally up to you;
It depends on how much time you're willing to do.
Can you feel the weight of my point?
Isn't the idea to avoid going to the joint?

Take care when turning volunteers away at the gate,
Some may actually be able to carry the weight.
You want to have fun while sitting on top
Because your fall will be impossible to stop.

You will become infected with hate and pain
Hoping for help from the few friends you might retain.
So think about your choice long and hard
Or you'll be picking your friend in the prison yard!

2/1/13

ONE LAST RIDE

I've gone nowhere at one hundred miles an hour.
Pushed my soul for every ounce of its power.
Tried to outrun memories infected with pain;
Causing a mass resurrection within my brain.

I now have an entourage of ghosts, demons, and witches.
Hidden no more, crawling up from mental ditches,
Victims I tried to bury secretly in my mind.
Have rushed forward refusing to stay behind.

Should've cut them loose to lighten my load.
Fear creates confusion and I'm running out of road.
They've driven ya away, making my world black.
I feel them grabbing, pulling me off the track.

I sense you're out there, standing just beyond my reach.
I hear your voice shouting "should've practiced what you preached!"
Too late for brakes – my road has come to the end.
Headed now to Hell – without your love or my best friend.

2/3/13

MY HOLD

Once I held her in my arms.
I held her much too tight.

She struggled to take a breath.
I held her much too tight.

She had no room for growth.
I held her much too tight.

She began plotting her escape.
I held her much too tight.

She was gone one morning.
Broke my hold and escaped one night.

2/3/13

LOST

Wish we could slip away alone somehow,
To erase the distance we have between us now.
What wouldn't I give just to have you here;
To hold you tight would off my fear.

The stars aren't shinning bright and I've lost my way,
The light of your memories is covers by clouds of gray.
Lost and found then turned around asking why.
No straight answer in this world shaped by lied.

I miss your kids, running my fingers through your hair.
Tired of waking up only to find that you're not really there.
I thought I heard you whisper "everything will be alright"
So that a brighter tomorrow would push away the night.

My heart worn and weathered, I've been stumbling
Through lonely nightmares that keep my fears rumbling.
Light a candle so I can find my way back to your heart.
Place it in your window so I'll know on which path to start.

I've heard you say I'm perfect, sometimes not worth a damn.
I know you'll do the best you can with who I am.
Give me one last chance and if I miss,
I'll do as you asked and blow you one last kiss.

50th Birthday
2/9/13

OUR WORLD

It's a shame to see the world that meth has built.
Anyone who has ever used must share the guilt.
When you look around and see smoke floating up in a stream
Place your bet – everything you have – someone just burned a
dream.

People are effected in so many different ways.
One thing is for certain – reality always slips away.
Men seem to change and become brave,
Clouding their mind on the definition of misbehave.

Women lose weight at an alarming pace,
Then can't keep their hands off their face.
Children soon are raised one parent at a time,
While the other is in the next room doing lines.

Friends get together to party doing lines for fun,
The next day we hear how one shot another with a gun.
Couples try to make love, only to find somethings wrong.
Admit it, doing the drugs way to long.

I won't act like above all this I've risen.
Hell is the reason I was thrown into prison.
Couldn't fight off the temptations and became a user.
Lost my true love when my mood swings started to abuse her.

2/9/13

BYE

Hope this poem brings a smile to your pretty face;
Something I haven't been able to do since I feel from grace.
I know you want to get away from me so bad;
That idea alone has been driving me mad.

In tears I say goodbye, my emotions won't wish you well
My demons are preparing them for a trip to hell.
They arrived right after you baptized me with pain.
I want you to remember my tears with every drop of rain.

You dare to shed a tear; the fucking game was in your control.
Used it to bury my love and pride in some dirty hole,
Or did you put it in your trophy case marked as a victory?
Do you laugh telling new friends your weapon?

I'll return pictures, letters, and anything you have brought.
This to relieve the pain in my head where your memory is
caught.
Poems that may have been written to you will be destroyed;
They're reminders of emotions with which you toyed.

I'd say don't forget me but I'm sure that's been done
Since you've already moved to ruin another mothers' son.
Showing that smile while you dance ringing in freedom bell;
Someone should tell him that is the elevator to hell.

I'd love to see your reaction when it happens to your boy,
The encounter with a woman who will chew his heart like a toy.
Be careful where you place the blame - don't get offended.
Give her a big hug – she graduated from the school you attended.

Good bye to your kisses, the smell of your hair,
The taste of your skin. Damn we were a pair.
God damn Nikki – I've never loved like this before.
Now on your existence I must slam the door.

2/16/13

THE AWAKENING

I've said I'm sorry. I've asked to be forgiven.
All in effort to stop the arrival of the forbidden.
Enraged and fed with the sorrow of this man,
Revenge is the only agenda that fuels their plan.

Climbing up, out of an abyss, hidden deep in my soul
They begin a journey with vengeance its only goal.
With no emotion they're bound by no rules.
Challenging all women, playing them like fools.

Fighting for weeks, twenty-four hours a day,
Their voices echo in my head "someone has to pay".
Lying dormant until the heart has been attacked
Then awakened in anger and set to strike back.

They are gathering in numbers, getting drunk on hate,
My mind desperately using logic to guard the gate.
It took one woman to start this war,
With demons who believe every woman should be treated like

2/20/13

FRIENDSHIP DIED

As I watch two dogs fight over a bone,
I thought, I've done that over a heart of stone.
Knowing damn well I had plenty to share,
I acted like I didn't want anyone else there.

Finally at the point where too much has been said,
The point when you realize you're in over your head.
Here's where we steal an idea from the clown,
We paint smiles on our face to hide away our frown.

In secret we count how many tears we've cried;
The total always adds up to a friendship that died.
Thinking if the other would've wiped our tears dry;
We wouldn't have to face the world with a painted on lie.

Allowing pride to wipe our face dry;
Took the sparkle out of each other's eye.
Then moving on, allowing emotions to fade;
Pride will never admit to mistakes we both have made.

Again all alone, to ourselves, we speak the truth,
To the silence we mumble, the other gave us youth.
Deep inside we keep bottled up pain,
Making our soul a very empty and lonely domain.

Listening to rumors of where the others may travel,
History repeats itself, truth is not allowed to unravel.
We take off running only to stumble and trip
Causing our fall – The Death of a Friendship

3/4/13

TICK-TOC

Tick-toc says the clock on the wall
Not enough time to say good-bye to you all.
I've address the closest to me,
Asking that in their thoughts they allow me to be.

Tick-toc says the clock on the wall.
Life has closed in like a long narrow hall
Too late to stop and check behind every door,
At this point, even in love, I've become dirt poor.

Tick-toc says the clock on the wall.
Please believe me, with my last breath you name I'll call.
If by some chance things don't go right,
Pretend I'm in your bed holding you so tight.

Tick-toc said the clock as it fell off the wall.
If fate has it that tonight I must fall,
Tell everyone there was a heart deep within.
It became a casualty while I committed a sin.

3/7/13

<u>EXPLANATION</u>

Why am I full of hate? It's because you broke my heart.
Can't blame it on love although it was an important part.
You did use the words "I love you" to dissect my soul.
Butchering my reasons for living, thus accomplishing your goal.

One layer at a time you peeled away my protection.
Carefully destroying any hope for a resurrection.
Emotions nailed to their own symbolic cross,
In order to feed your ego with the idea that its still boss.

Your eyes began to glow while picking flesh from your nails,
Knowing soon you would be dancing on bloody entrails,
Warm and pumping life, it appeared before your eyes
The reason for all your deception and dirty little lies.

No longer protected but lying in plain sight
My human life ended when you took your first bite.
Thinking you'd walk away as if you did no wrong
When my dreams catch you, you won't be feeling all that strong!

3/7/13

A WARNING

Please accept my apology if the warning comes too late.
I've been over-powered by demons full of hate.
Cried, begged, and warned you a long time ago,
That how long I could hold them – I don't know.

Tried to keep my distance so they wouldn't see your face,
Building up their numbers at a very alarming pace.
Fueled by your laughter about throwing me away,
Deep inside my soul they now refuse to stay.

Awakened by the argument between my heart and my brain,
Hiding in the shadows as the teardrops fell like rain.
My heart wanted to believe the look in your eyes,
My brain believed the look was nothing more than lies.

Now empty of emotions the demons have control.
Voices scream of vengeance for the damage to my soul.
If all of this becomes too hard for you to swallow,
They blame you for the man now emotionally hallow.

To those people outside now looking in,
Keep your mouth shut unless you're totally free of sin.
Believe me when I say I don't need you by my side,
Yet God help any of you bastards if you helped her hide.

3/14/13

RUNNING

I heard another friend's opinion today.
Like so many others he said "let her slip away".
He tried to remind me of the times you let me down,
How my smile was painted like that of a clown.

Listen everyone, for me there will be no end.
Not only did I lose my love but also my best friend.
My mind and heart have been torn so far apart,
Long gone are the smiles and kisses we shared at the start.

You blew my mind with your sudden run and hide;
A perfect plan that you executed with pride.
Sure it was easy to run with your hands covering your ears.
It going to be impossible to out run your fears.

Let me save you the trouble of looking back.
I am the crazy train running down your track.
Can you enjoy life looking over your shoulder?
All the while staying alert and getting older?

It's too bad that love is the birthplace for hate.
I do believe I've learned that way too late.
Now even friendship is dead and gone.
With my mind battling demons, to my love I wave so long.

3/18/13

HANDS OFF

Looking at my hands, they are battered and bruised;
On you they were never meant to be used.
Yet triggered by words they would fly,
Causing the sparkle in our eyes to die.

The words "I'm sorry" will never heal the pain.
Regret now is that fills every single vein.
Twisted and broken fingers serve as a reminder
During those lonely nights when I can't find her.

"I HATE YOU" were your last words by way of a text.
They echo in my mind while wondering "what next?"
My hands want you to feel the pain of my heart.
My heart blames my hands for us being apart.

It seems I may have lost you for good;
My new companion – a dark figure with a hood.
An old friend who believes revenge is the best action;
His goal to create another fatal attraction.

True to form I see him but I refuse to listen.
I know exactly what my heart and soul are missing.
Having gained this knowledge way too late
I'm forced to reach for you from behind the loneliness gate!

Dedicated to Nikki
3/19/13

<u>VISION</u>

I wish you would look into my eyes;
See that no longer are they clouded with lies.
So many things have moved into view;
Most importantly my vision of you.

Names like Jacquie and Alyse dislodged from my mind.
Nikki is the name that got my love running blind.
Over two months I've been starting for your touch;
As time moves on the pain is becoming too much.

No one seems to believe the words I write;
I wipe away all my own tears at night.
Is it only my love that has been replaced by regret?
How can it be so easy for people to forget?

Never before has my soul wanted to die.
I apologize to any of you if I've ever made you cry.
It feel like the end of my world draws near.
Sorry but my good-bye you won't hear.

Is that your voice saying "I don't care?"
I believe we could be a powerful pair.
We could stop these tears from forming rivers;
You could help me stop these shivers.

3/22/13

TEAM WORK

Taking turns shakin' the bottles until tight,
Then release the pressure so it cures right.
One friend after another works up a sweat,
No, no, no, it's not fuckin' ready yet.

Everyone wants to lend a helping hand,
Even a couple people you just can't stand.
Guys busting balls about who won't keep pace,
Silence falls over the room as a woman takes their place.

I think it's ready - the bottes getting hard.
Hell no, no wonder you've got your rooky card.
Everyone having trouble with the stamina test
Each trying to impress by doing their best.

Closing in on the two hour mark of shakin'
Arms so sore they feel like they're breakin'.
Ok it's ready to hit with gas,
Then through filters carefully – end of class.

Let it lay out for a while to dry.
The fumes can make anyone cry.
In a small pile grams of white gold.
Share divided and the rest is sold.

3/24/13

FALLING APART

Gone are the urges to hold each other at night.
It seems that energy is now used to fight.
"How did the world get so wrapped in turmoil?"
A thought as one passes the other a tube and foil.

It's become such a struggle to be kind
Suspicion at the back of each other's mind.
Once they were the best of friends,
Slowly another friendship ends.

Another future that's been tripped up and caught,
Silenced little by little with every package bought.
Pretending everything will work out fine
One wrong word and you're standing on a land mine.

Now they lay down to sleep but it's back to back
Both lying, thinking "when did things go off track?"
Awake throughout the night to watch the sun rise;
Inside their soul empties emotions as it dies.

Blind casualties of an epidemic without guilt,
Trashed are the dreams love had built.
Deep are the scars worn on each heart,
Still loving the other but forever apart.

Dedicated to Chacho and Nikki
3/24/13

LOST-N-FOUND

This rare moment is so you can read my mind.
No guarantee you'll like anything you find.
It's in a state of confusion about all it's been taught,
While drifting aimlessly by Satan it was caught.

You leaving left me without a sense of direction.
Temper now fueled with Satan's resurrection.
Pursuit of you has become our only goal,
Remembering first things first – pre-dig the hole.

Thinking of you every single day and night
Pits my heart against my mind in a daily fight.
Each day that passes causes my soul to become silent.
Louder are the voices of my demons becoming violent

Satan is waiting for the moment to be right.
Patiently my demons wait in the shadows of night.
Don't be afraid. I love you. Can't you see?
Those are the words I remember you saying to me.

3/26/13

DEMONS DANCING

I can't sleep with these demons dancing in my head
Some wearing faces of people I know are dead.
Over my dreams a black cloud has been cast.
Have they come to capture my soul at last?

Never wanting me to feel real joy,
Discarding my heart like a broken toy.
Their hands cover my mouth so I can't yell
While they laugh and drag me to hell.

My hands reach out grasping at hope
Only to be tied up with Satin's rope.
My dreams always seem so real.
Satan and I playing "Let's Make A Deal".

Once again felt love in my hand
Only to filter between my fingers like grains of sands.
The demons have reinforced all of my fears
Turning all of our happiness into tears.

3/28/13

THINKING

Cried again today at the mention of your name;
A pain filled heart reminds me I'm not the same.
Tears run down my face on their way to the floor;
Each one a reminder that I don't have you anymore.

Thoughts reflect on our happiness at the start
When we surrendered the love held in our heart.
Simply holding my hand made any load easy to bare.
Whispering "I love you" and that you felt same with me there.

Time allowed karma to have its way with you and I
Creating a negativity that caused our love to die.
Words became sharp as razors cutting away ties
Tongue became twisted tying knots with lies.

Now you're gone and my future has gone dark
My voice echoes your name like a lonely dogs bark.
Sleeping cold and empty my soul isn't well,
Cried again today for dragging you through hell.

3/30/13

<u>GOD & DEVIL</u>

Well that's just fucking great! She's gone
No shit, it's obvious something went wrong
How the fuck did you get to rue up there?
We ain't never got along, so I really don't care.

Then there's your buddy, the ruler of darkness
The deal I made with him made my life a mess
Is it true, you cast his ass out of heaven?
I met the son-of-a-bitch around the age of eleven.

Let me say that you two assholes are confusing folks
More and more I think people are believing you're both jokes
Constantly trying to prove who has more power
As lives like mine, right before your eyes, go sour

Sitting up in heaven all arrogant and smug
Making you an identical twin to any street thug
And you down there, sneaking around in the dark
They have scary creatures at the petting park

You two idiots need to stay out of human lives
Then we'd have happier husbands and wives
Children could learn of love and be friends
But what would you assholes do if the fun ends?

4/16/13

WHISPERS FROM OUTSIDE

It is so funny how you outsiders love to offer your advice
All of you trying to sound so sincere, honest, and nice
Could any of you walk the path of which you preach?
If what you loved so very much was paced beyond your reach?

No one on this earth can answer "what is love"
A riddle giving to us on earth from someone up above
It would be so much easier if he'd shout out his advice

I feel the pain deep in my heart from the lesson I have learned
Now stand here alone because of the bridges I've burned
It's hard to understand that love was born from pain
If not handled with care it'll drive a man insane

My past is littered with so many painful mistakes
Life on earth doesn't allow for perfection for God sakes
Why does my pursuit of you set off so many alarms?
We did have some special moments in each other's arms

God himself proclaimed that all sins could be forgiven
That our belief in him would keep us driven
I'm so tired of having to struggle each and every day
I believe God has his favorites with which he loves to play

4/25/13

FAKES

Speak up, did I hear you mumble a word?
No problem talking behind my back so I've heard
You cowards thought I'd never hear your lies
Now you avoid me; grow some balls between your thighs

I trusted you bastards by telling you all how I feel
In return you started rumors that from you I would steal
No one forced your dumbass to smoke all night long
Misplaced your drugs; again the same old song

The truth is you whores and junkies just can't say no
Slowly your addiction began to rapidly grow
Who started the rumor about the black dancer?
That right, why ask you? Only real men could answer

You want an example of honesty you bunch of bitches?
I'll be honest – fuck all of you at the house of snitches
To those of you who have told my love a lie
I wouldn't shed a fucking tear if any of you die

What a tragic waste of time trying to be a friend
Let's see who you fuckers need in the very end
Keep believing I don't know who you are
You're a celebrity at the local bar

6/2/13

A QUESTION FOR GOD

If there is a God in heaven, I'm asking if he'll listen
The happiness in my life for years has been missin'
True friends have been few and far between
Fifty years of age with love three or four times seen

Let me ask "why did you allow me to be born?
Did you get a laugh when my heart and soul were torn?"
I'll never say it was the worst, yet a painful existence
Then you handed me to Satan with very little resistance

Was that because I was a burden you didn't want to carry?
Knowing loneliness not death is what is truly scary
Haunted by demons as I look up out of my grave
The burial of a memory no one want to save

My body surrounded by the shadows from beyond
Breathing became difficult as dirt got piled on
Awakened by my fears and gasping for air
The undertaker wore a disappointed stare

Now I have to go, Satan doesn't like us talking
He prefers to be the creator of dead men walking
My boots are bloodstained and the soles worn
A questions for you "why was I born?"

6/4/13

<u>STORM</u>

Listening to the thunderstorm that has surrounded me
The lightning flashes as if it wants me to see
Rain falls onto my skin; the raindrops are cold
A sign that my soul is empty so I've been told

So much anger has built up inside
Emotions have fallen victim to genocide
All chewed up and then discarded with spit
My heart told my body it might be time to quit

I'm sure some wish I'd disappear
Then others could quit living in fear
Ironically it is I who may be afraid
What will be the price for the mistakes I've made?

Words now have the value of trash on the ground
Knocking on the gates of hell, hope can be found
Way too late to ask "what do I do?"
My final breath will be caused by you!

6/4/13

INSANE

I have a prayer for you sitting up in heaven
We lost touch since I was about eleven
My mother kept her faith in you throughout the years
I've always wondered why you never dried her tears

Witnessed love when father drug her down the stairs
Thinking "what a way to show he really cares"
My only child was taken by his mother by a guard rail
Her way of pounding in my coffin's last nail

My life has been derailed by all I've seen
Made a deal with the devil that only made me mean
I never wanted love to ever get a grip
Too much pain when emotions lose control and slip

Four years ago our eyes shared the same ray of hope
Never thought my heart would be dangling from a rope
How many times must I lose her tenderness before I learn?
Maybe God's plan is for me to crash and burn

Yet I'm gonna trust my mother and her faith in you
I'll leave it to your power to show Nikki my love is true
It's been so hard living with so much pain
With your help I can prevent going off insane

10/10/13

BETRAYAL

Betrayal, in itself, is a crippling force
Throwing its victims blindly off course
Never would you believe friends are involved
Overwhelming is the pain when the mystery is solved

How could their friendship have ever been true?
Flashing back through the past searching for a clue
You were there when they cried and were afraid
To support their decisions or plans they had made

Remembering the promises they wanted you to keep
Secrets that would be buried so deep
You felt the pain of their tears, tried to make them smile
Walked beside them every inch of every mile

Reality cuts so deep they don't feel the same
To them, al they've done was participate in a game
Only a fool breaks the loyalty code
Fuck them and the horse on which they rode

10/21/13

ANOTHER APOLOGY

I'm sorry that you feel the way you do
Life's been damn confusing for me too
Just when I think I'm doing a little better
I find myself so far away saying "go get her"

Off I go, a fool with no direction
Doing almost anything for a drop of affection
The words "I love you" have worn a path on my tongue
Send from a mind and heart no longer young

Days and nights move quickly into the past
Reminding me that life is passing so very fast
The choices of my life litter my path
Evidence used by karma and her wrath

Inside there are whispers that feed my fear
They arrive with the words you speak and every tear
You say I don't know who you really are
I agree, since you won't let love travel that far

My hold on life at fifty has begun to slip
You peel my fingers to loosen my grip
Happiness dies a little with each passing day
My only prayer is that you stop pushing me away

1/5/14

ABOVE THE REST

Well, got your way right to the end
The perfect plan; I'm not even a friend
Thank you for the painful lessons I've learned
Feels like my entire world has burned

I would bet you haven't shed a tear
Being who you are, there's nothing for you to fear
Practicing on me so you can council our youth
Do you think you'll be teaching them to tell the truth?

Will you explain that using people is an art?
That it is not against the law to break a heart?
This world is full of fools who are willing to give
Paying for school, computers, phones, or places to live

Saying "I love you" once in a while goes a long way
Happiness comes with deciding how they can stay
People like you make the world a better place
Teach them arguments aren't face-to-face

Most of your victories have come by phone
At that distance everyone is bad to the bone
Get them ready for release, they'll be missed
Never revealing that by Satan you've been kissed

1/20/14

POOR BOY

I wonder at times where you might be
Who your fooling and to what degree
Bet he fell for your eyes and that smile
Following you now like a puppy, mile after mile

Poor son-of-a-bitch doesn't have a clue
He's in for hell when you show him the real you
I'd warn him but it's probably someone I know
So let him suffer like an inmate on death row

Have you told him about reporting by telephone?
That you don't have to because you're grown
"I need some money" is what he'll soon hear
What you'll spend on him won't buy a beer

He'll be invited to holidays you consider yours
Any other time you'll tell him "go to your whores"
When you believe he's been used up dry
Like a coward you'll say its over with no reason why

He'll stumble around with his empty soul
Trying to add the cost of everything you stole
Yes, I wonder where you might be
Then I look up and thank God I'm free!

2/6/14

BLACK-N-SILVER

Our world wasn't built by one man alone
Nor was it meant to serve as one man's throne
Black and silver are the colors we fly
For our children some have chosen to die

With pride we must call each other brother
Stand ready to defend one another
To those who may think of us as weak
Blame is your own when vengeance we speak

We protect our existence for those in our past
Forever we want their dream to last
Never look at a brother and think you're better
Highwaymen are equals down to each letter

Yes, the higher the rank the heavier the load
Never forget whose loyalty may clear the road
If threatened, Highwaymen will unite as one
Black and silver will be the colors that block the sun

2/6/14

DEMONS RISING

I feel a battle brewing deep within my soul
A resurrection of demons with revenge as their goal
Awakened by all the damage you left inside
The theft of my heart and the emotions that died

Now you continue through each day with a smile
While my dreams and hopes begin to rot in a pile
Voices in my head sent whispers to my ears
My demons want to be laughing and dancing in your tears

Let me make a promise I will not break
So you may learn, in love, you must give not just take
I want you to feel every ounce of my pain
Then maybe you'll understand I'm hurt – not insane

The words "I love you" are not part of some game
I promise my dreams won't be so easy to tame
They want you to spend each day looking over your shoulder
Realizing loneliness only makes you grow older

Next time you're thinking of a love that been lost
Ask yourself "really…who's to blame for the cost"
Since my demons refuse to ever be left behind
I'm sure you'll realize they've infected your mind

Once again my soul has become the birthplace of hate
Thanks to you my demons have gathered at the gate
Thought I'd try to prevent any escape
Handed you my heart with your decided to rope

Now they are demanding to be set free
That it is you who is guilty in the first degree
Only wanting to express their love
Every fist dressed in a black leather glove.

2/15/14

188

GIVING UP

Say something - I'm giving up on you
I know that's what you want me to do
To walk away is easier said than done
The heart gets tangled in memories of fun

Say something – I'm giving up on you
Listen when I say my love was true
If I can't hear the whispers of your voice
I refuse to allow loneliness to be my final choice

Say something – I'm giving up on you
Couldn't look me in the eyes to say "we're through"
I will find the strength to turn and walk away
My fear is that in my past you will not stay

Say nothing – I've given up on you
The tears have dried like the morning dew
Time to travel down a new track
Fighting the urge to stop and turn back

2/11/14

<u>LETTING GO</u>

Another poem to help cleanse my battered soul
Scrambling to replace the emotions I thought you stole
Alone, once again, to wade through a sea of tears
The silence and loneliness are my greatest fears

I have no children to hug me at the end of my day
No wife or girlfriend to whisper "everything's gonna be okay"
Clouded are the memories of love flowing like a stream
I find it now impossible to even have a dream

Protective emotions have been torn away strip by strip
By a man-made beast that over the years has tightened his grip
Causing battles in which I pushed to you all the blame
Late only to be the one swallowing nothing but shame

Accused you of thinking you were perfect in everyone's eyes
You were only trying to rescue me from the beast and his lies
In reality my emotions you were not trying to steal
Actually they were what you salvaged from the ordeal

I must say I'm sorry for all your lonely tears
That I wish I could return what you call wasted years
Please continue to love me deep inside your heart
Without you mine is missing its largest part

2/28/14

<u>BRO</u>

So you want me to call you brother
That you got my back like no other
All my secrets can be trusted with you
At my side no matter what I do

I call and you don't answer your phone
Once again stuck and on my own
Leave a message is what I'm told
That damn recording is getting old

What a brother I've got at my side
It's starting to look like one of us lied
So where are you really? Some titty bar?
Or riding passenger in some boss' car?

Lets use as an example Cain and Able
Brothers who couldn't sit at the same table
I'll be careful calling you brother
Because one of them killed the other

3/2/14

SLAPPED

I never lied when I said "I love you"
Believed all your words were also true
You'd go off to work, me waiting for you to arrive
To enjoy that moment of feeling alive

How did I suddenly fall from grace?
Kissing replaced by slapping my face
The bruises were abundant, the slapping more frequent
Punishment for whatever you felt delinquent

Is that what I deserved for the love I gave?
Would've love you right into a grave
Now I'm gone, I will not be disrespected anymore
No more names like bitch, rag, or whore

I will find the strength to stand tall
Shouting to the world "I'm worth something after all!"
You can beg, cry, or yell for me to come on back
Too little too late – my trains traveling a new track

I'm headed where I can enjoy a sunrise
I will not sit alone wiping tears from my eyes

Dedicated to my friend
3/2/14

MY PEN

If I'm asked who's my friend – my ink pen
Knowing all I've done and where I've been
Putting into words how I may feel
Telling no secrets, now that's a deal

We've never argued on what I should write
For others it sheds a little light
Explaining what I have done and why
Someday I'll be dead and gone, it too will die

Helping to unravel the confusion in my life
Yeah at times just as dangerous as a knife
The ink has become my ammunition
With it I make each transition

It has moved very close to my heart
To work at keeping my soul from falling apart
Always expressing what I have to say
Never complaining about the time of day

Everyone needs at least one true friend
Especially in a world where so much is pretend
Over the years our bond has grown
Yet rest assured every word is my own

3/3/14

SEARCHING FOR A FRIEND

In this world we're taught to be suspicious of others
Overlook no one is what we're taught by our mothers
Suspicion was meant for protection but it's often a seed for doubt
We begin believing friends are something we can do without

In a lifetime we will find friends are few
Our minds will be blown by some we thought we knew
They will fall victim to life, liquor, or drugs
Greed has also turned good people into common thugs

Forever will come and go before you find the perfect friend
Yet somewhere there are those with whom you can blend
Disappointment will be the victor from time to time
You'll find deception between friends is the ultimate crime

Failure, loss, and bad judgment all have lessons to be learned
Those that can avoid these pitfalls will have a trust well earned
The search will be long and the risks are never fun
Remember to find a best friend you must first be one!

3/24/14

A.V.

Remember the years when we were the others one and only
It's still your voice that speaks to me when I'm lonely
Respect and admiration toward you keeps you above any other
Making the love in my heart for you second only to my mother

Even with so many regrets I keep you safe in my mind
So you can force me to slow down when I decide to run blind
I've created so much pain with things I've done or said
My time with you kept me from becoming emotionally dead

Can't imagine my world without seeing your smile
Of course there's your one-of-a-kind unforgettable style
Surviving alone in this world takes all my might
I have those night when I can't seem to find the light

I've apologized thousands of times while sitting alone
With every tear that falls I'm reminded the blame is my own
There entangled in my loneliness – your pictures I sometimes
hold
It warms my soul kept cold by secrets never to be told

Yes some have tried to occupy your space
They never seem to be able to handle the pace
Maybe I should be honest right from the start
Saying only mom and you have access to this heart

Dedicated to Alyse
3/14/14

TURN MY WAY

Will you ever look in my direction like you use to do?
When my words "I love you" really meant something to you
Many things have changed since way back then
Today our thoughts seem to fade with remember when

Most of my yesterdays have been easy to forget
Thankfully the memories of your smile haven't abandoned me
yet
Time will never allow us to reclaim any of the past
Nor does it give any clues how long our life may last

Many times I've wished I could travel back
To track down the emotions you say I lack
We both know that was only wishful thinking
Brought on by all the tears we'd been drinking

The present will prepare us for what might lie ahead
Only if we listen and learn from what has been said
There will be times we don't like what we hear
Honesty requires for both of us to be perfectly clear

In the past I may not have known how to act
Humans can never be perfect and that's a fact
Judge me on what I attempt, for failure is to never try
Everyone is entitled to find happiness before they die

5/21/14

<u>PLANS</u>

Why has this happened to me?
It's not how I planned for it to be
My life was going to be happy and fun
Never did I imagine me as the lonely one

Started full of energy and ready to explore
After my first taste I wanted more, more, more
Paid no mind to what was being said
Every time I climbed out of a different bed

Emotions abandoned or picked clean
Creating a human with demons unseen
Whenever I'd move forward they'd pull me back
Piling my mistakes into an overwhelming stack

We can take shelter under "I'm sorry" just for so long
In time it will collapse under all you've done wrong
With no warning the distance between love and trust has grown
Plans have changed, I've been left all alone

6/8/14

<u>ON TRIAL</u>

Go ahead keep bringing it; I'm starting to enjoy the pain
Forget the voice of reason, it's easier to be insane
I've cried, begged, and said "I'm sorry" at least a thousand times
Starting to believe you find joy in reminding me of my crimes.

You say violations of the heart can never be repaired
That they never would've happened if I'd really cared
In my defense my mistakes were never ever panned
Only to occur when you'd avoid the touch of my hand

No one finds comfort when love turns and walks away
Except for hidden demons who believe it's time to play
Your rejection started a war between my heart and mind
Now within my soul peace I may never find

So go ahead and be mean to me, cover me with dirt
Don't act surprised that it's with disaster I now flirt
Go ahead keep bringing it; I'm starting to enjoy the pain
Don't forget I once loved you and you drove me insane

6/25/14

FALLEN BROTHERS

For our fallen bothers who now gather on the other side
In our souls you will travel wherever we may ride
We offer the promise to help your families with the pain
For under our watchful eyes they are welcome to remain.

To those who don't understand how the losses make us fee
A bond is built on the highway riding horses made of steel
At eighty miles an hour, words are replaced by look
Within our eyes you can find the contents of a book

On rare occasions our thoughts may overflow
A window of opportunity, to where few are allowed to go
You may see a world ruled by an iron fist
We believe it's a world where respect still exist

Fallen brothers who now gather on the other side
Each of your stories help fill our souls with pride
We all have pages that are rarely seen
Camouflaged with sentences while living in-between

9/9/14

A LESSON IN BROTHERHOOD

For years we've trusted one another
To the point we call each other brother
Over time something within you changed
Your value of brotherhood had become deranged

It seems for year we've been blind
You had only your best interest in mind
Handshakes and promises tighten your grip
Slowly our scales of democracy have started to tip

Confused, some have no idea on which side to stand
Things seem to be working just as you planned
In our past right has risen and prevailed
Where will you stand when your plan has failed?

Will you be on the outside looking in?
All alone dreaming of what could've been
Or will you be on the inside looking out?
Wishing you would've learned what brotherhood is all about

9/25/14

SELF DESCRIPTION

My skin holds back so much pain
No cure, not even a storm of holy water rain
A tender touch would only burn my skin
Nothing been the same since the devil moved in

Fifty years it has taken to reach this point
The most peaceful part of my life – five years in the joint
So many I have hurt; so much I have done wrong
Some have said deep in hell is where I belong

No longer do I hear soft whispers in my ears
My hearts ben taken captive by pain and fears
All thoughts have become angry and confused
Poisoned by emotions battered and abused

Forced to exist in this world of lost-n-found
Where the discarded misfit toys litter the ground
Haunted by memories of victims left in the past
Casualties of a world moving way too fast

11/15/14

<u>LIFE STORY</u>

No one to tell my stories to
Where my life started and all I've been through
Now up in years and facial hair of grey
I guess I should be thankful for each passing day

Grow up in the country and played sports in school
No time for an education, too busy being cool
Tried going to college but I had a shortcut in mind
I'd hit the streets running, my fortune I would find

Welcome to the jungle where you learn to survive
Life is a raging river into which you must dive
Doing whatever it takes for each gasp of air
When it feels like your drowning, you ask God to be fair

Wasted so many years trying to get in
Now I find myself trying to forget where I've been
Sometimes at night I'm haunted by my choices
Shadowy face and their ghostly voices

I've accomplished to make very few friends
I'll probably be married to karma when life ends

Yes, I've committed some sins that are beyond repair
At fifty-one, the guilt is almost impossible to bare

12/16//14

SO THIS IS CHRISTMAS

What did you want for Christmas? To make this man cry?
With the freedom to use only motive, method, or lie?
The pieces of my heart already wedged under your nails
Serve as proof that love isn't the one that always prevails

With a smile, I'm sure you've mapped out your path
Leaving behind gifts booby trapped with games of wrath
Knowing damn well I'm the fool that follows behind
A victim to every trap because love has me blind

Do you laugh when I step, trip, and fall on the ground?
Or is it the fact that down your path I still travel
I believe every game is rigged yet I still get sucked in
No matter how hard I play, it's set so I can't win

Must be your fans I hear standing to cheer
Every time my eyes release another payback tear
Someday my eyes will close and the tears will dry
Is that gonna be the day you hope my love dies?

My love for you refuses to loosen its grip
Forcing the rest of me to survive the trip
People say I've become another casualty of war
That in this world is money not love that matters anymore

12/22/14

<u>CHANGES</u>

Sitting still while demons paint on another smile
They dance and sing of sadness, revenge, and denial
Enemies of my soul that I've kept locked deep inside
The painted face makes it easier for them to hide

Slowly taking over the emotions of their new host
Preparing for the birth of another empty and volatile ghost
My eyes no longer see love in the same way
The demons have causes everything to be suspicious and gray

In time the body will become numb to a gently touch
The loss of a love, in time, can cost way too much
Misled by my heart and mind in the past
Made it easy for the demons and the spells they cast

Taking back myself from them is so very hard
It's like that first talk through the prison yard
All eyes watching you for any sign of weakness
Straight faced you walk bravely with a touch of meekness

Like a virus the demos have continued to spread
A battle must begin before my heart is forever dead
I'll force them back from where they came
Then bandage my wounds and get back into the game

12/26/14

A TRAIN RIDE

Emotions with vanish as the room fills with smoke
The beast laughs louder every time you start to choke
He welcomes you to the reunion of self-pity and pain
The standing entertainment aboard his runaway train

Before you know it at the station of numbness it arrive
Here you ignore the pleading and crying of affected lives
To feel above all this you grip tighter to your chemical host
Unaware that eventually the ride will cost you most

Saying it's not your fault that the world doesn't play fair
Pretending to be tough, turning your back to those who care
Loved ones will begin pointing their fingers at you
Shouting that someday you'll find only their love is true

You'll then begin wondering if love could be that real
The question haunts you while you smoke your next meal
Could the truth be that of reality you've become afraid?
That pride won't let you admit to the price you've paid

You must let the smoke clear from your brainwashed mind
There is no shame in admitting the beast had you blind
It takes strength to break from the beasts' powerful force
It's a battle that starts deep inside yourself, of course

12/30/14

Chapter Seven

Tragedy

As any wise person knows, even the most straight and narrow life has its own tragedies. After Alonzo's disengagement from his former club, he acquired a new found lower profile. Yet, it has not been an exception from the rule. And some of these tragedies have been very tough to take for him.

May 13th, 2014, his very close friend, Taboo, was killed when a truck struck him while riding his motorcycle. Taboo had become Alonzo's mentor. Alonzo admired his friend for his unshakable way that he always looked at both sides of a story in every situation. And Taboo always reminded Alonzo "Anyone can make enemies. The trick is to make friends. That takes a brave man." With his past dealing with some serious betrayals, these words from Taboo resonated with him in very strong ways.

The second, possibly the hardest, was the loss of Jersey. Jersey was Alonzo's best friend and brother as well as former bodyguard. Alonzo and Jersey had been discussing their former club and the decisions that had been made, and Jersey was talking about possibly leaving the club and joining Alonzo, joking that they were "both just getting old".

On October 14, 2014, after staying at Alonzo's all night, talking about old times and plans for the future, Jersey was hit while riding his motorcycle home and killed. His death left a deep scar on Alonzo.

Early 2015, Alonzo rushed into an emotional battle to the aid of his friend, Josh. There had been a time when Alonzo, himself, knew about battling ones own demons all too well. Josh was waging this exact war. However, on March 21. 2015, Josh lost the battle and was lost to his internal demons forever.

All of these deaths would take him back to his past each time, including the memory of his friend, Runner. And Alonzo wrote poems for each of these men as he processed all he had gone through with them and where their loss left him. Once again, he found solace and therapy in his written word.

THOUGHT ABOUT A FRIEND

Allow me just a few moments of this day
I want to speak of a friend who has gone away
A man who waked softy down is own road
Whose words were sincere with every story he told

Never speaking of enemies but of friends he had
Saying that evil thoughts would only leave you sad
Explain that you must work for anything you love
And never be too proud to ask for help from above

Only foolish men believe they need no one in their life
Once telling me "he never would've survived without his wife"
Saying anyone can make enemies, the trick is making friends
Believing tomorrow starts the way the previous night ends

Well my friend let me say a few things about you
I'm so very proud to have ridden with Taboo
Your works of wisdom I will share with anyone who may ask
I'll tell them you were a real man, never hiding behind a mask

I remember you telling me wisdom comes with age
Do the best you can then simply turn the page
I guess this is where I'm supposed to say good-bye
I say "I'll be fine" would simply be a lie

To Taboo – so long my friend
5/19/14

FAREWELL FRIEND

With regret we bid farewell to my best friend
Jersey, a Highwayman, right down to the end
Many miles of road we spent side by side
Anywhere, anytime we were ready to ride

Our friendship was never up for debate
Often we sat and spoke of our fate
No matter what anyone may have heard
You judged men by the value of their word

A loving husband and a devoted dad
Often stating you were lucky to have what you had
Bet your last dollar leaving wasn't his choice
Listen to the silence and you'll hear his voice

All these years we trusted only each other
You, my friend, knew the meaning of brother
I made a promise to you a long time ago
A promise that only you and I know

Now to your family I would like to say
Our souls have bonded on this terrible day
Of this man you should all be proud
He walked softly and yet his steps were loud

To those of you who didn't really know him
The chance of meeting a better friend – zero to slim
I refuse to say goodbye, I feel you standing there
With your Cheshire the Cat grin and soul piercing stare

Dedicate to Jersey – RIP
10/20/14

TRYING TO UNDERSTAND

In Oklahoma a young man said good-bye
Here a family gathers trying to understand why
It's strange how peace can be hidden by pain
Or that within a loss there may be something to gain

We have all searched for some peace in our soul
Only to be surprised that there's a price for that goal
We must unlock emotions to explain how we feel
Admitting to the world we are not made of steel

We must also learn to listen with our eyes
For it is much harder for the body to tell us lies
Actions most often reveal more of the answers we seek
Lies can be well hidden by the words we speak

If we must also find a resting place for blame
Lets blame a life that conceals the rules of the game
This doesn't mean that it's impossible to win
Victory will arrive as happiness from within

From the pain of our loss we must learn all we can
Starting with: the weight of the world is too heavy for any man
Unfortunately life doesn't come with a guarantee
Nor will it ever offer anything for free

Dedicated to Josh
3/28/15

RUN FOR FREEDOM

Can you afford the price to play?
The life of a friend was what it cost today
Shot while he was trying to evade
In the ground his body was laid

He refused to return to a cage
The streets had become center stage
Five years of freedom had finally past
The curtains drawn, show time at last

His secret revealed by some dirty snitch
I bet you can guess, it was some bitch
Marshals gathered to Lansing for a chase
Hoping to cover every last base

In the end the government won
All those agents against a gang of one
Friend, with us, you made a name
Runner: all pride and no shame

In memory of Runner – 1960-2005 – Rest in peace
2/11/05

<u>Chapter Eight</u>

Reformation

Over the years, Alonzo not only continued to write, but he also reflected back on his earlier poems. They were a lesson and a reminder of where he had been and where he didn't want to go back to.

He has come to realize that the people that have helped him the most in his life went through the least of his troubles with him. Yet they were the ones that were there for him when he needed them most, even when he was at his lowest.

As time goes by, he has worked to lead by example. He's taken all that he has learned about the meaning of keeping one's word and has instilled it into a less dangerous and more upstanding life.

It's not been an easy road for him. He battled his inner demons frequently as well as his own anger. However, looking over his past and reading his works help keep him grounded as well as serve as a reminder of where he doesn't want to go back to.

Over the years, yes, he started leading a far more straight and narrow life. He adapted the ideals that he can't expect anyone to do anything he, himself, wouldn't do. And he spreads the lesson of standing up for what you believe in and being true to the promises you make wherever you can.

NEW YEAR'S RESOLUTION

Yes, I've decided on a New Year's resolution
It's to cleanse myself of your emotional pollution
Thank God the big picture has started to clear
Have you always run from things that you fear?

Then you build defenses with my past convictions
Allowing you the time to make your well planned predictions
Clinging to every mistake I've ever made
You intentionally set out to make sure each is repaid

What I can do you've proven you can do better
Because when it comes to revenge you're a real go getter
I used to hold you so much higher than most mothers
Until you started acting like you were better than others

I think you've kept me on a leash just in case
You're confronted with something you'd rather not face
You become so kind with your beautiful smile on display
With the problem solved you again push me away

1/1/15

<u>WHY STAY</u>

Let me tell you I'm sorry that you feel the way you do
God damn life has been confusing for me too
Whenever I feel like I'm doing a little better
I find myself alone reading another "Dear John" letter

Once again a fool traveling in every direction
Soul thirsty, searching for a drop of your affection
"I love you" rests patiently on a dry tongue
Heart pounds, mind spins for they are no longer young

Day and nights move quickly into the past
Reminders that life in general is moving so fast
Choices I've made with life now litter the path
Obstacles that help make up karma's wrath

Facing your back makes it difficult to hear
The words you may be speaking as you shed another tear
Shouting that I don't even know who you are
I do know that in my world you're the only star

Do you want me to admit my mind mas started to slip?
That as fifty-one I can't seem to get a grip?
Mind, body, and soul die a little bit each day
Truth is that without you, why should I stay?

1/1/15

JUNKY

You don't see them during the light of day
At night they're looking for a place to stay
It's a gypsy way of life chasing their next high
Pretending this is normal, believing their own lie

From snorting to smoking now hooked on the shot
Keeping from the world this new habit they've got
Once they find a private place and only they remain
Now comes the smile while picking their next vein

The beast has hooked another victim with his liquid charm
With sweet anticipation he arrives entering through the arm
The fear of needles has been chased away
Like the thought that infection will arrive someday

Noting better looking than a needed in the vein
Believing it's the cure for any type of pain
Now locked away somewhere shooting up their dream
Showing no regrets about their looks for self-esteem

Then one day while staring at a mirror
They'll be introduced to a stranger with eyes full of fear
The conversation will be a lie, how all things are good
Standing behind them, a dark evil image wearing a black hood

1/5/15

EQUALS

Women demand equal pay, equal right
Equal opportunity and to be heard.
That I believe is all fair.
Why doesn't that apply for men in relationships?
Equal say, equal rights, equal opportunity
And to be heard.
If either wants to be heard both should listen.
One doesn't need to speak down to the other.
Emotions just as valuable on either side.
Shady is shady on either side.
If we can't pay by the same rules,
Let's start over with might makes right.
Winner makes the rules.

1/6/15

DO YOU HATE ME?

Do you truly hate me in such a way
That you wish to avoid me each day?
Knock, knock, knock. You won't answer the door
Inside wishing I wasn't alive anymore

I can't describe how my soul cries
At night the tears drown my tired eyes
Your words of pain echo in my head
I hear "I hate you and wish you were dead"

No longer does the future look so bright
Loneliness haunts each and every night
There is no happiness in waking up alone
Constantly checking the ringer on the phone

Lost are the answers for those who ask why
Can they see the emptiness in each eye?
Wish I could force you to let me back in
Or remind you that no one is free of sin

Do you truly hate me in such a way
That you believe there's a debt I must pay?
Knock, knock, knock. Come answer the door
I don't want to hurt you anymore

1/7/15

A PRAYER FOR HELP

Why won't you answer me when I pray?
Is it because I've taken a life away?
Damn it, listen to me like you have others
Although my faith may not be as strong as my brothers

Would you rather I get down on my knees?
Raise my hands up to the sky begging please, please?
Throughout my life it's been test after test
Was it because I wasn't as good as the rest?

Can't you hear the screaming escaping from inside?
The sound of a wounded soul betrayed by pride
It's telling you it may be bleeding to death
The loss of love could be its very last breath

I'm not the fool asking for monetary wealth
I need discussion about my emotional health
Isn't it enough I've been denied children and a wife?
Or is this how you feel I should live my life?

Of you, Jesus once said "ask and you shall receive"
Did he speak those words only to deceive?
Your very own son was nailed to a stake
Yet forgiveness you offered those men for their mistake

She's walking away and I hear your laughter
Is that because there is no happily ever after?
I want the forgiveness you've given other men
I want the protection you gave Daniel in the lion's den

Speak to her about my love and her denial
Let me once again put sunshine in her smile
Do not allow our future to become a fatality
Because you allowed our imperfections in all reality
Dedicated to Nikki
1/7/15

INSIDE SECRETS

It's never been easy to cry
For each tear someone had to die
Another secret like the lightning rod
Representing someone is buried in sod

Rumors the media has kept alive
Symbols that only the strong survive
The tattoo becomes a label or a brand
Displayed by those with blood on their hand

Washing the hand by looking for change
An attempt to put the past well out of range
Unlike the sinner, a memory is forever caught
With its ability to infect even the smallest thought

Memories that can accompany a person everyday
Create nightmares that sleep can't wipe away
The sinners can smile and act content
Yet in hell their lives will be spent
1/12/15

THE MOTH

Is it just me or does anyone else
believe relationships are mimicked by
nature through the actions of the
moth. They must reach the source
of the light. The fact it may be a
flame doesn't alter their course.
Bravely they continue their fight
only to parish and seize to exist.
The flame has no remorse and
continues to feed. It doesn't realize
that it is the sudden bursts of
light that actually make it so
attractive.
1/19/15

FOR ARTHUR

Our proud family has lost another son
My question, why Art? He never hurt anyone
When I sit and think back onto my childhood
He's always there where the memories are good

Quiet as he was, he was someone I looked up to
I could always depend on his concern to be true
He once told me "A real man admits when he's wrong"
That his faith in God kept him strong

I know you dealt with your own share of pain
Making sure that on your feet you'd remain
You believed that wisdom would come with age
Saying life is too short to fill it with rage

I hope you'll understand if I don't say goodbye
We'll meet again because someday I too must die
It doesn't matter when, I'll know where you are
Sitting on a couch up there paying your guitar

1/28/15

<u>WINDOW</u>

Life has become a scene out of Shakespeare
Forced to observe a lost love from here
In a small room asking for answers from above
What must I do to reunite with my love?

I stood at the window, a smile and then a frown
Loneliness arrived in a tear rolling down
Broken calloused hands wiped my cheek
Once powerful now empty and weak

The strength I received from your touch
Is the reason I miss you so very much
Peering out the window like a prison gate
My thought "have I learned this lesson too late?"

Apologies I have whispered over the years
Included "I'm sorry for all of your tears"
Each carrying pain you didn't deserve
The memory a life sentence I must serve

Outside the window the total of mistakes I made
Clearly you were the greatest price paid
Regret dancing in my soul hurts so much
Like love, the glass ice cold to the touch

2/4/15

LONELY BIRTHDAY

How should a person celebrate a lonely birthday?
By telling themselves that in twenty-four hours it goes away?
Then try to stop the mind from hitting reverse at high speed
No one knows what you want, yet everyone tells you what you need

Avoid visiting disappointment from the past
Don't make excuses for good things that didn't last
Never forget the memories of moments that went bad
Your wisdom grows from the experiences you've had

Should we be glad we've gained another year of age?
Our chapter in the book of life has gained another page
Making it longer than the chapters of some unfortunate others
Some of those being fathers, mothers, sisters and brothers

The edge of loneliness is sharp and as lethal as a knife
It has scarred me many times throughout my life
Forever will it be impossible to predict a lonely birthday
Yet when it arrives we can make it end in our own way

2/9/15

BACK FROM SCHOOL

When will you put an end to this game?
The moment I accept all the blame?
How deep do you want me to feel the pain?
Think you can handle me going insane?

You've left me in this dark, lonely abyss
Are you sure you want to torture me like this?
Leaving my broken heart in the hands of Satan
Knowing my hopes and dreams will also be taken

Watching from behind a shield of children and friends
Are you hoping my pursuit of you now ends?
Right now you should have only one thought
"Have I learned anything from the lesson you've taught?"

I heard you laughing while you put me through hell
I'll be the one laughing when Satan opens my cell
Free to leave his lonely emotional prison
Open your eyes to a new demon risen

Thoughts of you are forever locked in my head
Sure I've been locked in hell but I'm not dead
Misled by love, your weapon of choice
Your poison delivered in your words and voice

I hope you recognize me upon my return
I'll remember you caused my future to burn
Well, well, well – look who slipped past hell's gate
I've arrived straight from Satan's classroom of hate

2/9/15

GOOD-BYE

I believe your dream has come true,
The dream where I say good-bye to you.
Hopefully your soul fills with joy
As mine lies on the ground like a used up toy.

Good-bye to your kisses and your touch;
The pain on holding on has become too much.
My mind has wandered valleys and stumbled up hills;
Couldn't control the pain with powder or pills.

Now at rock bottom, all stepped on and bruised.
Once a proud mad lies heartbroken and used.
With such damaged emotions can anyone survive?
Can their respect for love be allowed to talk or dive?

None of this is for you to worry about.
You got exactly what you wanted and that's out.
I refuse to believe it was all just pretend,
Yet it's a shame our friendship has to end!

2/26/15

<u>NEVER A FATHER</u>

So it appears I'll never be called father or dad
Putting an end to the greatest dream I ever had
Never to announce I have a daughter or a son
God, is this punishment for the things I've done?

I have brothers, sisters, nieces, and nephews
All hold a spot in my life, hopes, and views
My brothers and sisters are fathers and mothers
So the children that surround me all belong to others

Am I to believe that a father I will never be?
Was it you God who cut my branch from the family tree?
Our tree has blossomed so very well
My branch needed to fuel the fires in hell

Well, when my fatal day arrives and I must die
Please wipe my tears before closing each eye
Proud to have been my mother's oldest son
Yet never knowing the pleasure of a wife, daughter, or son

3/8/15

SHORT TIME

I've looked out my window countless times
Tears of regret remind me of my crimes
Gently wiping my eyes before turning to face the guard
He announces that it time to head for the prison yard

Stepping from my cell then to standing in single file
Continue facing forward, eyes fixed on the floor tile
Arriving at the exit I'm blinded by the sun
Its warm rays deliver forgiveness to everyone

Always careful not to lose touch with reality
Because inside the fences there is no sympathy
My mind in overdrive as I return to my cell
Thinking no longer will I fear walking through hell

Sitting on my bunk I begin thinking I'll survive
Remembering it won't be over until home I arrive
I picture dad, mom, Nikki, and Chach waiting
Already I can hear the last two debating

There goes the dinner bell, but all thoughts on hold
Glad it's almost over, tired of doing everything I'm told
I can't wait to see my cats or smelling country air
What keeps me optimistic? Mom and dad both will be there!

Dedicated to Dani
4/6/15

WHAT HAPPENED

A man and woman both so very strong
Yet lacking knowledge about getting along
Their lives had survived moments in hell
Creating so many secrets neither could tell

Brought together while searching for love
Feeling forgotten by the man up above
Thinking they would be safe in one another's arms
Letting themselves fall victim to each other's charms

They had finally found what they were looking for
A bright future with only good things in store
The years took their toll while moving so fast
Minds became infected with memories from the past

A wounded soul created bleeding from her heart
She believed to heal it would take a new start
The tenderness of his touch had become a violent grip
A reaction to his fear that love was starting to slip

She simply went back to what worked before
Telling this man she didn't love him anymore
Not believing his pain because of a violent past
Haunted by demons and the shadows they cast

Laughing and drinking helped while turning her back
Not wanting to witness his crazy train leaving it track
Soulmates, lovers that were once called friends
Have now become enemies as their world ends

What will be the outcome when the smoke clears?
Two casualties with broken hearts and eyes full of tears
New students of a lesson brought on by life
Remember, sometimes our past can cut like a knife

Dedicated to Chacho and Nikki
4/26/15

3 DEMONS

Well, well – look at you all cocky and free
Now that you're exactly where you wanted to be
My soul became just another casualty left behind
Thankfully its ghosts will forever live in your mind

That quick shadow in the corner of your eye
Is one of my demons acting like a spy
He'll always be standing in the darkest spot
His target is the guardian angel you've got

Lying in the dark all alone in your bed
Suddenly a memory begins moving through your head
Another demon of mine with sharpened claws
Trying to escape from inside your mental walls

Suddenly you feel a temperature change
You've just entered another demons range
Then you feel something touch your skin
It almost feel like something's trying to get in

All are happy that we ended with hate
Allowing them passage through hells gate
Well look who finally got what they wanted
And now we'll both forever be haunted

6/6/15

NEVER AGAIN

Never again will we lie next to one another
You simply found comfort in the arms of another
Finally you can feel safe when you sleep at night
Sleeping next to someone you want holding you tight

I know I'm the last thing on your mind
Replaced by the joy of leaving me behind
Now you ask "where did the last eight years go?"
Wasted time and wishing you would've said no

With a new soulmate to drag around town
The ex has a smile painted on my a clown
Looking over your shoulder can't be much fun
You also decide when, where, and how we were done

People surround themselves with who they want to be
So they can also act out exactly what they see
Things worked out well, sticking me with the blame
You painted everyone a picture and used me as the frame

I won't say good-bye or wish you the best
Hoping you meet karma while out on your quest
I'll be sitting here studying my defeat
To give you my opinion the next time we meet

6/8/15

<u>RAGE</u>

Holding back the rage that's been born inside
A child of victimized emotions that have died
Secretly moving through veins to remain hidden
My heart says vengeance must be forbidden

Rage feels when you're near and blood begins to boil
Circulating inside like the bodies motor oil
My mind sends orders to each awaiting hand
The heart still argues nothing ever goes as planned

Chains that once joined our hearts have begun to snap
Rage continues flowing into the widening gap
Now you do your best to avoid my infected blood
While all along you've drug me through the mud

Blood now heated and infected beyond repair
Rage is convincing the mind to just not care
Heart exhausted from trying to keep the peace
I thought it was love, to you it was just another lease

6/5/15

MIND YOUR BUSINESS

Yeah, yeah, yeah – your mouth says you care
Believed that once and no one was there
People have said over and over "she's not worth it"
Let me respond by saying "mind your own shit"

For me it's not so fucking easy to forgive
Fuck with my emotions, I don't want you to live
You forced me to let go reluctantly
My mind has a plan that ends more destructively

Once again people say I should rise above that
You'll accomplish more with flowers than a baseball bat
My question is "whose side are you on and for what reason?
Because from where I stand it sounds like treason"

I don't need any of you to shoulder my pain
Let me warn you that I'm a runaway train
I'm not fooled by any false anticipation
On a carriage driven by the devil, only a fool asks its destination

6/10/15

LET GO PLEASE

Why can't you love her and say goodbye?
Have you ever felt the pain when you've made her cry?
She's hidden her world in an emotional mist
Knowing you have a devil in each fist

Let her go before your memories are erased
Before they're filed where hate is placed
If you must continue to stubbornly refuse
In the end it is you who will ultimately loose

Wanting her to pay because your soul feel dead
Why can't you see that her soul has also bled?
A hell like this cannot be created alone
You had help for inside you a devil has grown

The devil has drug both of you through hell
Thinking both your souls were his to sell
Do not listed as he whispers in your ears
He is the manifestation of all your fears

His influence has driven her so far away
With no remorse he'll hurt you everyday
Let her tears dry so she can move ahead
She takes you along as memories in her head

6/12/15

A LONELY FRIEND

Listening to the disappointment in your voice
I already know what would be my choice
Once upon a time you only had doubt
Hoping the truth you would never find out

"I love you" you read with your very own eyes
How many other nights did he fill you with lies?
Pride does its best to keep you so strong
Inside your soul reminds you that he's done you wrong

No escape from the thoughts that make you feel used
Searching for a cure to sooth emotions abused
Finding yourself in bed, it's dark and you're very alone
Your mind decides to create a fantasy of its own

Wishing you could rest your head on your friends shoulder
Then wrap his arms around you to keep from getting colder
As you look into his eyes he reinforces your trust
Safe are all your secrets along with fantasies of lust

You feel his hands caressing your skin
Then your body decides to let your friend in
For so long you've been missing being so wanted
Until it happens your mind will be haunted

All of a sudden there is the sound of an alarm
Once again you awaken with no one on your arm
You get ready to face the day the best you can
Maybe even turn your fantasy into the perfect plan

Dedicated to Tiffany
6/29/15

I LOVE YOU A LIE

My heart loved you so much it set you free
My mind blinded by hate just can't see
The words "I love you" are the perfect lie
Liars use them to look you in the eye

My heart wants to treasure memories of you
My mind blinded by hate believes a penalty is due
The words "I love you" are the perfect lie
They can fool the heart into another try

My heart holds a picture of the smile on your face
My mind blind by hate pictures you in a different place
The words "I love you" are the perfect lie
They leave their victims asking why

My heart wants the taste of your last kiss to survive
My mind blinded by hate doesn't care if it's dead or alive
The words "I love you" are the perfect lie
An infection that causes emotion to die

My heart crumbed as you walked away
My mind blinded by hate caused my heart to pay
The words "I love you" are the perfect lie
Still never as painful as your words good-bye

6/30/15

DOWNWARD

How can I stop this downward slide?
Loneliness is becoming almost impossible to hide
Lying in bed staring at the ceiling
Amazing how silence can be so revealing

Thoughts float in from every direction
Most of mine seem to have an infection
Caused by memories that've escaped the past
Nothing will grow in the shadows they cast

I will not shoulder the blame for lives that were lost
They entered the game knowing what it could cost
Yet they are allowed to disrupt my dreams
Cutting the threads holding me together at the seams

Anytime I find happiness or something good
My past arrives dressed in the Reaper's Hood
It has cost me love, children, and a wife
By not allowing any of these to enter my life

Over twenty-five years since they last asked why
Their memories tattooed under my eye
We all had our shot at rolling the dice
Who knew they would deliver my price?

7/2/15

BEYOND REPAIR

Blood flows as I tear you from my mind
Trying to destroy every memory I can find
Losing the battle to your venom in my blood
Caused me to drown in your hatred flood

Not a day passes, even now, in my life
That I don't feel your tongue sharp as a knife
Watched you kick my world all over the ground
Echoes of your laughter are now the only sound

The words "I hate you" spill easily from your mouth
My "I love yous" have also gone south
You continue the act of being so tough
Hiding the coward who runs when things get rough

It's such a shame all's gone to hell
That we have no sweet story to tell
Once we held each other's heart
Now even friendship is oceans apart

7/3/15

<u>REFLECTION</u>

Come a little closer and I'll tell you who I fear
Believe it or not, it's the man in the mirror
For years I've tried to escape his grip
His control has cost me so much on this trip

He's made promises to camouflage his lies
Hiding betrayal in those cold empty eyes
When you question the evil he has done
He convinces you it was done all in fun

Mind and heart feel so very betrayed
For it is to them most of his promises were made
My soul was billed for the lies they were fed
Payment caused it to be emotionally bled

No longer do I dare gaze at that reflection
Those eyes hold memories of a painful direction
How can I find someone to love and trust me?
If even I can't trust the reflection I see

7/25/15

FREEDOM GATE

Stop talking like you and the beast are cool
To him you're just another addicted fool
He lets you believe that you're the one in control
Making it much easier for him to reach his goal

Tempting people in many different ways
Starting by keeping them awake for days
Patiently waiting to infect your soul
Inside he'll undermine reality like a mole

Emotions, judgment and self-esteem become tired
Casualties of a life that has been hard-wired
Eventually the addiction nears its final stage
When you place yourself in a paranoid cage

The reality you once knew will have disappeared
The person you've become is someone you have feared
Thank the beast for the addiction you've got
Yet he doesn't care if you survive or not

Is this really how you want it all to end?
Believing the beast was your only friend?
Start fighting back before it is too late
Do whatever it takes to reach the freedom gate

7/25/15

NIGHTMARES

Who will awaken me from my nightmares?
Or understand the truth each one bares?
Lying next to me you protected me from ghosts
Your understanding is what they feared the most

Late at night since forced to sleep alone
Loneliness sends chills through the bone
Body becomes covered in a cold sweat
Nightmares arrive with memories I've tried to forget

With nothing to fear they come and go at will
One after another like a well-rehearsed drill
Battering my mind with regrets from the past
Blanketing my future with an eerie overcast

Sometimes I awaken lucky to get away
Other times in the nightmares I'm forced to stay
On those occasions I miss you the most
For as an individual no man can defeat a ghost

Once again it's time to prepare myself for bed
I try to clear my mind of thoughts I may dread
Shut off the light and close my eyes tight
Hoping the ghosts allow me to sleep tonight

7/26/15

BATTLEGROUND

The smoke from the battle has started to clear
Giving hope to enemies that peace may be clear
Pain and regret now fill every footstep found
No longer is any place considered sacred ground

Boundaries once defined by fences of respect
Can no longer be found due to years of neglect
Gone are the signs of "Beware – Do Not Cross"
Increasing the chance of an emotional loss

Individuals who stood firm in what they believed
Created a tension from which suspicion was conceived
Diminished value was placed on each other's word
Doubt was reinforced with every rumor heard

Allowing the distance between them to pull them apart
Changed their status to enemies of the heart
With no respect for the other, they didn't talk anymore
Secretly gathering evidence and preparing for war

Finally when the sunshine went totally dark
And the only sound was a lonely dogs bark
The enemies both charged forward intending to win
Victory will be granted to the one free of sin

7/29/15

12 STEPS TO THE END

The party begins when the work is done
Nothing but friends and laughter on day one
Day two seems to blend into the first
Everyone satisfying a social thirst

Attitudes visually change by day three
People concerned only about me, me, me
Only veterans should pass into day four
Because reality isn't the same anymore

With dry, pale skin you'll enter day five
Here you'll ask yourself "am I still alive"
Thoughts become paranoid and fool the mind with tricks
The world spins you in all directions on day six

Thinking more dope would put you in heaven
Creates hell on earth as you arrive on day seven
Locking the breaks to avoid day eight
Face the facts your reactions too late

Wishing you would've never done that first line
Blame only yourself for being alone on day nine
You being trying to remember where you've been
You become a zombie at day ten

It's a little late to believe you're going to heaven
When you think it is day seven, in reality it's eleven
As you stare into a mirror at your only friend
On day twelve you decided to bring it all to an end

7/30/15

TWISTED

A waste of time is what you once said
On occasions you even wished me dead
You created a way out then you walked
By your own guilt you began to be stalked

Placing the blame on me helps you sleep at night
When you know it was you who didn't do me right
Telling your story with so many facts missing
Receiving sympathy from those who will listen

Painting over the facts of who you really are
Then polishing any that might make you a star
The justification you've decided to use
Is some fabricated story of so much abuse

Are you gonna continue with your distorted lies
Until every ounce of love for you dies?
Should I find joy in how you must hide?
Or that your freedom won't start till I've died?

8/1/15

<u>TEDDY</u>

I woke up this morning laughing at myself
I dreamt this old toy had been put on a shelf
Feeling like an old teddy bear left on the bed
Who is now used to prop up someone's head

I like to remember when I was brand new
Should I mention the nasty things I was forced to do?
Now as time passes I spend more time alone
Because your options for toys has grown

Sure, you still need me when you're feeling sad
Trusting the oldest toy you have ever had
Asking me questions about what you should do
Thinking about what I'd like to do to you

Silently listening as you explain how you feel
Hugging me as if you believe I am real
Wishing we could be so much more
Then comes a younger toy and I'm on the floor

8/25/15

<u>DISCONNECTED</u>

The number you have dialed is unable to take your call
You wonder, would they have taken it at all?
Not wanting to believe what you heard on the phone
It would force you to face your greatest fear: being alone

In your loneliness confusion will kick open a door
Behind which happiness was left dying on the floor
The air in the room is filled with questions, memories, and fears
The floor is stained and slippery from salty tears

Even when no one answered I'd continue to speak
Hoping to receive the elusive forgiveness I seek
I'd leave messages never expecting to hear back
Even those empty calls keep this train on track

A general recording couldn't ever answer why
Coward you are not, so don't use it to say good-bye
It's been years since we really have connected
Since that first bruise happiness became neglected

This poem is a message that may never be heard
I am still seeking forgiveness, give you my word
The number you have dialed is unable to take your call
You wonder, would they have taken it at all?

9/12/15

DAY DREAMING

I'm at a loss for words to describe how I feel.
Didn't think I had any heart left to steal.
With a subtle precision you slipped under my skin.
Even after I swore no one else would be allowed in.

Like an addiction you've taken control from the inside.
When I try to shutdown, thoughts of you push override.
Wounds that were left open and infected
Finally have started to heal and feel protected.

Captivated by your questioning eyes and sweet smile,
\My mind insists that you're there each step of the mile.
I've thought of holding your hand walking in a park,
Wrapping my arms around you when the world goes dark.

Yes, my better looks and years are things of the past,
But it takes a toughness and wisdom for a person to last.
Let me shield you from any unforgiving pain.
Keep focused on that elusive happiness that drives me insane.

Perfection is not what I'm trying to sell.
I offer wisdom collected while living in hell!
I bring a loyalty that has become a rumor,
What some consider painful, I call humor!

Dedicated to Tiff.
11/20/15

SUICIDE

In silence we'll face our greatest fear.
Loneliness always finds us when no one is near.
It begins to dig up memories of happiness once had,
Once again our emotions are confused and mad.

Thinking nothing can set us free like death could,
Its popularity, to me, has become understood.
When your mind can't control emotional pain,
It starts believing, in life, there is nothing more to gain.

This is when your body starts feeling lonely and old,
Causing your heart to go numb and cold.
The mind continues thinking about the freedom offered by death,
Then it begins weighing the value of that last breath.

Does anyone care how many times you've cried?
They won't even act concerned till after you've died.
Forgotten are the moments you reached for a hand.
Lying, they' say, they didn't understand.

Why bother saying a single good-bye?
So they can pretend to care by asking why.
In the dark thoughts of death bounce in your head,
Since only loneliness now shares your bed.

11/30/15

WAKE-UP AND WRITE

I was awakened in the middle of the night.
You were in my dream and asked me to write.
The words you spoke to me sounded so true,
You told me you'd love it if the poem was for you.

Yes, I will write anytime that you ask.
In the warmth of my words allow yourself to bask.
I have never allowed such access to my soul;
Gambling with emotions could take a heavy toll.

You've entered the armor of this lonely man of steel;
I believe you know exactly how I feel.
More than once something special has passed me by.
What would it take to become the sparkle in your eye?

In the past poems of hate were easier to write.
Your eyes and smile have brought me into a different light.
With that tender voice that fills my demons with fear,
In my dream you said "Chacho come here".

Neither of us knows what the future may hold.
We both deserve to be happy before we get old.
I think of you more than once a day,
And in my dreams, forever you're welcome to stay!

Dedicated to Tiffany
12/6/15

ADVICE

My poetry has been used as a bandage for years.
I've used it to cover wounds and wipe away tears.
The expression of emotions is said to help heal.
What if we're beyond knowing how that may feel?

I've written about love, hate, and even death.
Spoke of angels, demons, and smelt satan's breath.
The damage to my soul, at times, seems beyond repair,
Haunted by ghosts I know shouldn't be there.

A casualty of the war between my mind and heart;
I keep losing the people who can keep them apart.
They start out being soft and gentle, then become steel,
Only after their emotions have become my meal.

Tangled in a search for peace between happy and sad;
Lost in a world that drives so many people mad.
Then someone comes along as a glimmer of hope.
All I can see is a noose at the end of a rope.

At fifty-three, I'm running out of places too look.
I present my life in the pages of my book.
Avoid my footsteps, no one wants a man like me.
So open your heart, keep your promises and happiness is a
guarantee!

1/30/16

248

<u>Chapter Nine</u>

The Little Things

Alonzo's younger brother, Badge, formed a charity group called Bikers for Books in 2013. They gather books and monies through direct donation and events to get books out to school aged children all year round.

Believing that reading is an integral part of learning, they work hard to make reading fun for kids. As of 2016, the group continues to grow and take on more and more projects. And Alonzo is not only involved, but he's humbled by and proud of his brother. There's no question that Badge has found his calling, and Alonzo works hard to show his support for that dream.

He wants his brothers to know what he has gone through and not to follow in his footsteps. He wants them to understand that shortcuts and easy ways are often the longest paths in life.

Alonzo has come to believe that everyone really does want to love and be loved in return regardless of their past. However, he understands that one's past dictates many aspects of one's present, and it truly dictates when and how a person will love.

It's amazing what we all take away from our experiences. Through all of the lessons he's learned and all of the things he's gone through, sometimes it's the little things in life that have stuck with him and remind him of the man he wants to be. It's that mug with the steam rolling off of it, listening to his grandfather talk about life while sipping his morning coffee. Those are the moments we all go back to when you're thinking back on life the most.

But most of all, one things he has learned and wants to teach others is this one last thing:

"Truth and wisdom come with age."

The Poet:

"Three can keep a secret if two are dead

But those two remain buried in your head

Because we know the secret is never really over

Until all three are covered in clover."

-Alonzo "Chacho" Gomez

From "A Secret"

About the Author:

Colleen Nye

Colleen Nye is the author of several novels, including The Unattainable Series, Immersion, The Lunch Time Anthologies and The Long Summer. She writes in various genres as well as owns Blue Deco Publishing.

Working on From Pen To Page was a new concept for her. Despite being versed in various genres, she'd focused on fiction. Venturing into helping write Chacho's biography was a welcome adventure for her on many levels.

Currently, Summer of 2016, she's circulating in the convention circuit, signing books for her fans as well as working on an upcoming paranormal series, the second of The Lunch Time Anthologies and book three of The Unattainable Series.

You can follow Colleen Nye here:
ColleenNye.com
Facebook.com/AuthorColleenNye
Twitter.com/Colleen_Nye
Instagram.com/AuthorColleenNye

Acknowledgments:

I would like to acknowledge my friend Wende Pepper who painstakingly helped put my words to paper, thus Pen to Page. Thank you!

Sincerely, Alonzo Gomez "Chacho"

www.ingramcontent.com/pod-product-compliance
Lightning Source LLC
LaVergne TN
LVHW052017080426
835513LV00018B/2068